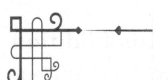

MW01036847

A Fool's Wisdom

Science Conspiracies
&
The Secret Art of Alchemy

"Dedicated to my wife Carrie, my daughters Ava and Neela, and my son Aro, the lights of my life, without whom this work would not be possible."

Steven A. Young

Preface to the Second Edition

A wise old master once said to me, 'The first thing you learn when you publish a book, is all the mistakes you made.' Well, eight months have passed since the publication date, and the illuminating light of awareness has penetrated every nook and cranny of the manuscript. Every sentence scrutinised with unrelenting tenacity. All grammatical and syntactical impurities isolated, eliminated or transformed.

If you were negatively affected by the parsimonious use of full stops, inconsistent apostrophisation, or inappropriate capitalisation, the time has come to rejoice! The rectification process is complete. The book has been gently fermented, distilled for eight lunar cycles and sublimated with a purifying fire, separating the proper from the improper, the subtle from the gross. A multitude of minor modifications have amounted to a major modification in the writing style, improving the sentence structure and advancing the articulation of the prose.

As a music artist, I wrestled with perfectionism frequently. I'd spend far too much time obsessing over tiny details and trying to polish every microsecond to an impossibly high standard, causing projects to drag on and on forever. With the book, I knew I couldn't possibly make it flawless. I am just a man, a humble fool. The important thing for the first edition was to get the message out, to just say what I needed to say.

In the months leading up to the publication date, there were various pressures to contend with. I decided to publish on April 1st 2024, Fools Day, the 64 year anniversary of the first-ever televised photograph of the globe earth (page 74). But it also happened to coincide with the day that the Scottish government enacted their dystopian new 'hate crime' laws, designed to protect the woke establishment from criticism and scare people into silence on important issues.

Given the somewhat contrarian leanings expressed in the book, I half-expected to publish and be met with a knock on the door from the thought-police. Thankfully that hasn't happened. Nobody is getting arrested for writing books yet, only for stickers, tweets and Facebook posts.

Hundreds of people have written to me in the months since publishing. None have yet come forth in defence of atoms, gravity, heliocentrism, evolution or viruses. Instead, several physicists, chemists, doctors, lawyers, entrepreneurs, podcasters, artists, alchemists and healers have expressed their emphatic gratitude and support for the words herein. People really are waking up from a monstrous scientific deception, and it's multi-disciplinary.

Awakening is what happens when a dream comes to an end. That moment when we open our eyes, and the cold light of day washes out the hallucinogenic theatre of the hypnagogic state. Though the word 'dream' is defined as a 'sleeping vision', it comes from the Germanic word *draugmas*, meaning 'deception, illusion, or phantasm'. To awaken from deception, illusion, or fantasy, is called a **Rude Awakening;** the sudden and unpleasant discovery that one is mistaken.

Rude awakenings are rare. They initiate a profound transformative process, snapping us into a more neutral and detached state of mind, from which we can evaluate our conditioning. The beliefs and assumptions we took for granted, the rules and dogma we were taught to follow. All of it is cast naked against the wall and doused with the icy waters of scepticism. False beliefs are blasted away, even stubborn clingers that have been rooted in the mind since infancy.

Truth is the signal, and all that is inauthentic or unreal becomes noise. Desires can simply expire. The material trappings we used to crave no longer seem to satisfy. There is a growing sense of 'divine unrest' as we are confronted with the burden of what to do with this newfound knowledge, how to operate in the world as a dissident, an ideological outlander.

What follows is both a catalyst and a companion for those awakening souls. Many readers have reported a total worldview transformation. This is not simply a book of alchemy, it's an *alchemical book,* designed with alchemical principles every step of the way. First to break down, dissolve and eliminate the materialist impurities that clog up our cognitive faculties, and second, to construct a superior scientific paradigm based on Aether and the elemental building blocks of Fire, Air, Earth and Water.

All love,

S. A. Y.

Table of Contents

Introduction
On Fools & Wisdom

Before reading a book, it is wise to learn a thing or two about the author. Though I could quite easily say I am this or I am that, and rattle off my career history, academic credentials, music discography, peak achievements and so on, the most important thing you should know about me for the purposes of this book is that **I am a fool**.

At the age of 46 now I am no longer a young fool, nor am I yet quite an old fool, but it's fair to say that I am a *professional fool*. I realise this may seem to be a self-defeating attitude, and there are those who think of me as some kind of a genius, but whilst I am grateful for such praise, I remain firm and without any shadow of a doubt that a fool is what I am.

Like with many words, what it means and how it is commonly used can be quite different. The meaning of 'fool' is quite nuanced. It can be used disparagingly for one who is slow, moronic, dumb or retarded, a simpleton or mid-wit.

But it also encompasses the joker, clowns, comedians, tricksters and jesters, one who is entertaining, satirical, sarcastic and contrarian.

I am not a comedian by trade, nor am I a simpleton or mid-wit, but I am certainly sarcastic, contrarian and an entertainer. My unconventional life path has brought me to an understanding of the fool as ***one who plays***.

This definition encompasses the music makers, DJs, artists, actors, dancers, comics, clowns, sportsmen and performers of all kinds. They're all fools. You see, the world is a very serious place, a sort of prison camp where we are expected to get in line, do what we're told, work hard, be productive, make money, pay tax, pay bills, take pills and so on. There's all kinds of troubling realities to contend with, like war, genocide, sickness, lies and betrayal, and worst of all death itself, which taunts us every day from beyond the grave. So a fool is really any one who stands boldly in the face of all that pressure and simply just *plays*.

By playing, the fool helps others to lower their inhibitions and relax into a more natural state of being, less affected by the oppressive conditions of worldly life. As a DJ for more than 30 years, I would get paid to go to events and play my music, fooling around on stage, performing, dancing, helping people to loosen up, to forget their worries and strife, to smile, laugh and dance and move their bodies in new ways. Deejays and clowns are not so different after all, they both go to work on stage in a circus tent with colourful clothes on, some even wear make-up, wigs and masks, but ultimately the whole point is to have fun and loosen up, to bathe in the good vibes.

Though music is great fun, I have always taken my art quite seriously, and approached it with a scientific, shamanic and alchemical perspective. The music is designed to be medicinal, to provide relief from pain and worldly tensions, to inspire movement and transformation, feelings of excitement and awe, wonder and ecstasy, to raise people into a mystical state of union where healing happens more readily, and epiphanies and life lessons are revealed. The aim with the music is to give people an extraordinary visceral experience that leaves them feeling recharged and *full* of good spirit.

When I say I'm a fool, I must clarify that I am not a trickster, I am a *sincere fool*. Unlike the trickster, I take no pleasure in deceiving people, playing pranks or watching others suffer and fall, I can't stand cruelty, lies and deceit, I have always been a seeker of truth with a desire to heal and inspire. I didn't always consider myself a fool however, that is a relatively recent discovery. I thought I was a very smart and serious person, because I am the holder of a Master of Science (MSci) degree and PhD in *Theoretical Physics*, making me an actual *Doctor*, a certified credentialed scientific expert, a bonafide **boffin!**

Impressive though it may sound, once I left academia the titles no longer seemed to have any real weight. There were no meaningful jobs and none of it really mattered 'on the street.' Once I went full-time making music, I became an independent artist, entertainment for hire, a real life *Disco Stu*.

From 2010 onward I pursued my music production goals with all the energy I could muster, releasing tune after tune, faithfully saying YES to every gig offer, travelling insane distances and playing to thousands of people in exotic locations, soaking in as much as I could in the process. People told me I was 'living the dream', and at times it sure did seem that way, but one thing they never tell you about living the dream is that all dreams come to an end with an **awakening**.

'If the fool shall persist in his folly he shall become wise'

~ William Blake

We see this character of the Fool as a central figure in the Tarot, also known as *The Book of Wisdom*, in which the Fool is the first card in the deck (technically the zero card, corresponding with The Joker in the standard playing cards). The major Arcana represents a spiritual journey, the quest for divine secrets and mysteries, and the Fool is the first step on this path to wisdom.

Occasional or half-hearted fooling around is not enough though. To really walk the path, one must be devoted, persistent, committed to their 'folly'. But 'folly' in this sense is not about being stupid, reckless, and unhinged, though it may very well seem that way to normal folk, it's about indulging your creativity, being playful and having faith.

The fool wears his heart on his sleeve, and is always depicted as a young man looking upward to the sky and about to walk off the edge of a cliff. This is a symbol of living authentically and faithfully, staying focused on God. He is also depicted with a dog by his side, 'dog' is of course is 'god' in reverse, the dog symbolises God because it is the best and most loyal friend a man can have. Dogs love us how we ought to love God.

In the native American tradition, the archetype of the fool is found in the spirit of the Heyoka, also known as the Sacred Clown. It is said that the Heyoka lives life opposite to everyone else in the tribe, wearing strange clothing and accessories, engaging in bizarre behaviour and rituals, as well as creating art, songs, and medicine. The Heyoka is not outcast for being weird and different, but accepted as an integral part of the tribe, serving an important function for the community.

Like a fusion of the jester and the medicine man, Heyoka provides an air of mystery, amusement, and relief, a friendly contrarian who holds up a mirror to the people by doing everything in reverse of the norm. In doing so, he serves the tribe in ways they didn't even know they needed, diffusing tensions and balancing emerging polarities.

The modern day musician/producer/DJ is similar in function to the Heyoka. He wears the funky outfits and lives a life contrary to the norm, he goes to work when everybody else is going to party and he sleeps when everyone else goes back to work. In its highest expression, the DJ fulfils a shamanic role within modern society, channelling new musical frequencies into the culture, a purveyor of altered states of consciousness.

In a traditional court setting, the fool plays a unique role as the only one who is allowed to criticise or make fun of the king, taking all the praise or the abuse, whatever comes. It is considered a very bad omen if a king were to kill his fool. The fool is seen as providing a connection to the divine and supernatural, as well as being popular among the laity, a close friend and confidante. Killing the fool means the king has some serious personal issues. He can't take a joke or handle criticism. It implies weakness and corruption.

When we look at the current world age, where the internet has become like the 'court' or 'public square', and social media platforms are the digital nations, it is clear that the fools have far more influence with their jokes, memes and music than the 'suits' have with their drab tiresome rhetoric. People need to laugh and cheer and dance, it helps us to process the emotions of life. Fools help to make life bearable, or better yet, enjoyable.

Literature has a lot to say about folly and wisdom, it's a fundamental axis of growth and an important polarity in story telling.

'The fool doth think he is wise, but the wise man knows himself to be a fool' ~ Shakespeare

Though modesty prohibits me from declaring myself wise, this indefatigable Shakespearean logic dictates that I *must* be wise because I *know* myself to be a fool.

Thus, I have become inescapably identified with the paradoxical **wise fool**. The beauty of this is that the wise will see me as wise, and the fools will see me as a fool.

Unconventional though my views are, they have become so crystal clear and strongly affirmed in recent years that I have been compelled to commit it to official record in the form of this book, to capture and convey what modicum of wisdom I have gleaned from my nearly half-a-century of life thus far.

For many years I thought the PhD was fairly useless, a meaningless accolade without application in the real world. Though there is one advantage that is clear now. It gives me a morsel of credibility with which to debunk and rebuke the false scientific doctrine that permeates the academic curriculum and popular media. Of course I realise credentials are not everything, but they are *something*. I would not be writing this book if it were not for my scientific schooling, which has implanted within me a moral duty to report on the results of this experiment we call *life*.

PhD stands for 'philosophy doctorate', and while the word 'doctor' is most commonly associated with MDs and physicians, its original meaning is something more broad. It derives from the Latin word *Docere* meaning 'to teach or instruct', as in 'doctrine' or 'document'. It was not specific to the healthcare industry, but represents a more general provider of truth, a wise master, mentor or guru who is learned in both spiritual and scientific matters.

By virtue of this mastery, he is able to create solutions, heal disease, and make things better for people. Early church fathers were called *Doctours* (13th C), but the modern use of 'doctor' to mean 'physician' was a convention that came about in the 16th century. Before that physicians were commonly known as *Leeches*, presumably due to the widespread use of the blood-sucking worms in healing applications.

Philosophy comes from the ancient Greek Philosophia (φιλόΣοφία), and is generally given two main definitions:

1. The study of the principles of knowledge and the nature of reality,

2. A belief system or codified way of living (creed).

Breaking down the word with etymology reveals the true meaning encoded within:

Philo (φιλό) = love or 'fondness of',

Sophia (Σοφία) = wisdom (goddess of)

Therefore, philosophy = love of wisdom.

From this analysis we can obtain a better understanding of the original intended meaning of PhD as a **wisdom teacher**, and it is my sincere hope that I can live up to that.

We may also deduce from this that the true meaning of an MD is one who teaches us to heal ourselves and live well. A medicine *man* is one who provides or administers the medicine, like your regular pharmacist or street dealer, but a medicine *doctor* should be one who *teaches* and *instructs* on the path of right living.

Though I'm not an MD, I have gained a lot of 'alternative' medical knowledge through my studies into shamanism, music and alchemy, through self-healing and raising three children as naturally as possible. I am also part of a network of alchemists, healers and naturopathic doctors who are, in my view, some of the best medical minds of our generation. So even though it was not the subject of my university degree, I have been studying and practicing natural medicine in my own life for over 15 years. I may not instinctively know the remedy for every malady (my wonderful wife has a far better intuition for that), but I understand the mechanisms of healing and how to seek natural solutions.

Actually the DJ functions in a similar role to the MD, they are both expected to provide relief from pain and make people feel good ... *and there's almost always drugs involved.*

The DJ is not a drug dealer however (that's the MD), but dance floors are usually packed with people who dose themselves with various psychoactive substances, natural and synthetic, and so the dance floor is a kind of alchemical forge where music and medicine interact in the crucible of the mind. It is a spiritual shamanic experience that can be profoundly healing when it's done right. People have been writing to me for years with stories and gratitude for the healing experiences they've had, it's what keeps me going with it.

Making music that people loved was such a contrast to my days as an office-dwelling physicist solving equations nobody cared about. There were a few occasions when someone said to me 'so you're a physician?', and I would have to say 'no, I'm a physicist', which begs the question, what's the difference? Well, it gives me no pleasure to say it, but the big difference between a physicist and physician is ... *physicists don't help people.*

As I will put forth in the following pages, modern physics is pure **sophistry**, a spiritual and intellectual dead-end, a fabricated worldview designed to obfuscate true science, glorify false idols and bamboozle the public into an infantile level of comprehension.

So let's get into it. There's a lot of ground to cover, I promise not to lead you astray, but as you follow me on this journey you may want to consider the question posed by master Obi-wan Kenobi when he said '*Who is the greater fool? The fool, or the fool who follows him*?'

Part 1

Science
Conspiracies

Chapter 1

Alchemical Awakening

In the fields of knowledge there is a distinction between higher and lower levels. Low-level knowledge is concerned with the intimate details and minutiae of the various day-to-day comings and goings, the nuts and bolts, the ins and outs, the juicy gossip. Whereas high-level knowledge looks over the system as a whole and deals with universal truths, governing principles, and the patterns and processes that sustain it. In order to integrate higher knowledge we must be *humble*, open and receptive. A keen student with a willingness to learn and do better.

It is harmful to the development of the soul if we cling to those beliefs with which we were programmed at an early age. We have to be able to recognise when a belief has been 'installed' within us by the surrounding culture, to be able to question and reprove it, understand why it is there, and ultimately detach from it if necessary. Purifying our inner landscape in this way is an important aspect of the Great Work of Alchemy.

In history we observe that humanity has gone through cycles of darkness and illumination, periods where knowledge becomes lost or hidden and things are bleak and savage, and then times when knowledge flows freely and there is a blossoming, a **renaissance**. Alchemy is that timeless illuminating knowledge, the science of creation itself, a wellspring of artistic inspiration that blossoms in the human mind producing great heights of civilisation, technology, and architecture.

Also known as 'The Art', I began rediscovering it around 2013, there is a copious amount of ancient literature on the subject and I will include many references throughout. I have only scratched the surface of what is out there, and can only imagine what is tucked away in old world libraries, but the Hermetic teachings of the Kybalion[1] and the Emerald Tablet[2] of Hermes Trismegistus had a profound impact early in my journey.

The knowledge filled my psyche like a ray of wisdom from the distant past, illuminating, nourishing and healing the mind. It purified my senses and my thoughts, exposing the errors in my mental conditioning, revealing the crude scientific dogma of my university indoctrination. In the light of Hermetic teachings, it began to look as though the whole canon of modern physics, which I was enamoured with for so long, was essentially a fruitless intellectual exercise, a mathematically justified fable installed in the minds of the populous and sold as the consensus explanation for *everything*.

This kicked off a solid decade of hardcore 'soul science' research, where I went fool-steam ahead into the world of shamanism, taking part in dozens of medicine ceremonies, visiting the interior lands of my own soul and rectifying, separating the gold from the dross. I revisited my science education with open eyes and it was plain to see the errors and malevolent agendas at play. Scientists often characterise alchemy as being "medieval proto-chemistry" but this is a very limited view. It actually informs and encompasses all the modern sciences, as well as being an

---

[1] Kybalion by Three Initiates
[2] Emerald Tablet, Alchemy of Personal Transformation by D. W. Hauck

endless source of inspiration for art, and a key to philosophy and scripture. It's better to consider chemistry as one of the *fruits of alchemy*.

Like a universal language, alchemy is a hidden gem that reveals secret connections and layers of meaning in all nature's wonders. It is not without merit to call it 'divine science' since in every culture where alchemy was practiced, its origins are attributed to divine beings, not human[1].

Positive Sciences

The term 'positive sciences' has been used to distinguish those branches of science which are based on natural phenomena, empirical evidence, and the use of the scientific method, from those which are based on mathematical models, metaphysical concepts and speculative ideas (they'd be the 'negative sciences' since they consume a lot of time, effort and money, but produce nothing of value).

Unlike the theoretical jargon of academia, which deals in abstract mathematical models and postulated particles, Alchemy deals with real sensory phenomena and practical creative knowledge, the kind of science you can apply at home, in your own way, for the benefit of your health, wealth, and that of your family and community.

Alchemy is the historical root from which all positive sciences stem. It provides a symbolic representation of nature that can be applied to any human discipline or creative endeavour, whether working with metals, herbs, music, video, paint, sculpture, literature, architecture, food, medicine, animals, even human beings and whole nations, all things are subject to alchemical operations. It is universally applicable to all types of work and is constantly active in sustaining life and creation. It is the science with which creation was made, **the science of transformation**.

[1] The Secret Teachings of All Ages, by Manly P. Hall

We are always participating in alchemy, like the fish that is always participating in water but does not know it. Our body is an earthen vessel, a biological laboratory of elements and processes maintained by the various systems, organs, and glands. Once we understand the language of alchemy, we can participate more consciously in its processes, bringing about positive growth and transformation through our creative efforts. Finding limitless resource and inspiration from the natural world.

Occult Curriculum

But just as we must research the ancient knowledge, we must also detach from, and unlearn, much of the modern science with which we have been conditioned since birth. For as we shall see, modern science is not the miracle we've been told it is. It has become a monster, a thoroughly discredited pack of lies and falsehoods. Modern science, or more specifically **Scientism**, is a *worldview* that is stubbornly committed to being godless, soulless, and spiritless, in spite of any and all evidence to the contrary.

Of course it's not exactly news that scientism is a godless creed, that has been the default scientific position since the 17th century. The denial of 'spirit' and 'soul' makes it anathema to Alchemy, to all spiritual and religious teachings, and even to creativity itself. Scientism is an insult to artists and anybody who ever had a spiritual or divine encounter, it nullifies your soul and invalidates all inner meaning.

The negative sciences in general provide no benefit to humanity, they are sustained only for the purposes of control and power. Their purpose is to hide true knowledge and distract people from ever seeking it (*its complicated, just trust the experts*). When false information is contrived for the purposes of hiding true information, this is **occultism**. It is a practice whereby powerful knowledge is concealed and sometimes 'hidden in plain sight' so only the right kind of person can see it.

Alchemy is occulted by both science and religion. There are religious zealots who will claim that alchemy is evil witchcraft, while atheists will claim it is a discredited medieval pseudoscience. As I hope to show you in the pages ahead, the real witchcraft is the mainstream media and the pharmaceutical industrial complex, and the real 'discredited medieval pseudoscience' is the state-sanctioned curriculum we were force-fed at school.

A Lesson in Humility

Alchemists stress the importance of humility, because a humble mind is always ready to receive higher truth. If we cling pridefully to false knowledge then truth will flee from us. We must always be ready and willing to have our worldview transformed into something greater and more illumined. We must be able to discern between the true light and the false light. To follow the golden thread.

Back in 2002, my PhD supervisor, a senior professor, told me a story which always stuck with me. There was an international nuclear physics conference back in the 1980s where all the world's top researchers gathered annually to share their work. One of the guests of honour was an old professor who had spent his entire career developing an exciting new theory of the structure of the atomic nucleus. Everyone admired him and was familiar with his work, he was a legend in the international theoretical nuclear physics scene.

During the conference, a young post-doc, fresh out of his PhD and still wet behind the ears, got up on stage to deliver his presentation. In it, he systematically debunked and disproved the professor's theory, using sound scientific methodology and reasoning, demonstrating that it could never happen as it was physically and logically impossible. He showed this beyond any doubt, revealing that the professor had spent his whole life promoting a theory which was inherently flawed and just plain wrong. The professor stood up from his seat, walked down the aisle, got up onto the stage and reached out and shook the post-doc's hand, saying 'thank you, now I know the truth'.

This story is a lesson in humility, and a reminder to all intellectuals that truth should always be the goal. We must be prepared to let go of our beliefs and admit fault the moment we become aware of it, even if we have spent our whole life working on it. It's the honourable way.

It can be difficult, embarrassing, humiliating even, as our ego gets attached to the wrong ideas. We may even be successful and financially dependent on perpetuating them. Nobody likes to publicly admit they were wrong. It is vulnerable, a form of surrender, a humbling. Humility is the opposite of pride, it's what makes an apology a real apology. If this professor were full of pride, he would kick and scream and launch ad-hominem attacks, demanding that the post-doc be cast out from the conference and stripped of his honours for daring to question authority.

Pride puts ego above truth, humility puts truth above ego. At its most extreme, pride can completely block people from the truth that is right in front of their noses, it's a form of spiritual blindness and a back-door for demonic influences to enter the mind and take over. Alchemical texts and religious scriptures are replete with warnings about the consequences of pride.

Whereas, humility is said to be a precursor for receiving higher knowledge and for effective healing and prayer, it's a key component of spiritual development. We must be able to humble ourselves before the eternal truth of the universe, or we are destined to live out our lives in darkness, believing in fables and pseudo-science.

Science as Religion

Scientism represents the sum total of mans best attempts at explaining creation without a creator. For this reason, it has become a quasi-religious doctrine in modern times, a sort of 'atheistic religion' with its own idols and dogmas, opposed to divinity in all its forms, and in full denial of the human soul or the creative (holy) spirit. But all practitioners of science are not necessarily impious. One of the so-called fathers of quantum physics, Werner Heisenberg, is quoted as saying *"The first gulp from the glass of natural sciences will leave you an atheist, but at the bottom of the glass God is waiting for you"*.

As a former quantum atheist myself, I can attest to this. Many people only take one gulp and never get to the bottom. Scientism is full of 'one-gulpers', but as someone who has drunk down every last drop, I can assure you there's no uncertainty in this principle. If truth is what we seek, then truth is what we shall find.

For those who wish to deceive people and exploit nature, scientism is an important ally as it provides the intellectual justification for evil. Scientism has no built in morality, fanatical believers can do evil deeds all day long with a clean conscience since there is no sin, no karma, no spirit, no soul, no after-life, no judgment, no creator, it's all just predators and prey, kill or be killed. A convenient creed for a death cult.

In opposing scientism, we are like David in the story of David and Goliath. But the giants we face are not flesh and blood, but 'isms' and 'ologies', decrepit doctrines that are propped up by religious authorities, clandestine government programs, and media propaganda. The difficulty in wrestling with these big ideas is that there are legions of determined believers who are attached to them like barnacles on a sinking ship, and we must endure their scathing abuse and vitriol while it all goes down. But this is an alchemical purification process in itself.

Science as Method

Let it be understood, all that is good and pure in science stands strong. What works, works. True science is impervious to criticism, it can't be debunked, it can only be smeared, obscured, and covered up. In essence there are three parts to the scientific method; observe, hypothesise and test, it's quite straightforward. However, to 'hypothesise' really means to 'use your imagination.' It's an educated guess, and it must be tested by designing, building and conducting experiments, which is costly, time consuming and proper hard work.

So there is a whole layer of academic science now that has abandoned observation and testing altogether, and instead just hypothesises all day long. This is theoretical physics, the *explanation layer*, where many of the concepts are intangible, unprovable, or just way beyond the ability of mere mortals to comprehend.

'Todays scientists have substituted mathematics for experiments, they wander off through equation after equation, and eventually build a structure which has no relation to reality.' ~ Nikola Tesla

It's true, I was one of them, guilty as charged. I wandered through the equations (I used to dream of equations) and built many a mathematical structure that had no relation to reality. The more exotic and complex, the better!

'Nobody that I know of in my field, uses the so-called scientific method. In our field, it's by the seat of your pants, it's leaps of logic, it's guesswork.' ~ Michio Kaku

It's no great secret, theoretical physics is essentially just 'explanation guessing.' They have cast the scientific method aside so as to untether from the constraints of truth and enter the realm of fiction and fantasy, a liminal zone where intrepid desk jockeys venture in their minds, highly prone to fallacies, falsehoods, and fudgery of all kinds. A zone where people like Michio Kaku permanently reside.

The scientific method was designed to ensure that all scientific work is fruitful and positive, that it can be relied on and built upon. This goes out of the window when it comes to theoretical work, and it's had quite damaging consequences on the civilian population who have largely come to trust in science as this infallible all-knowing institution that superseded religion.

After having spent the last decade unlearning all the science I was indoctrinated with, my conscience compelled me to tell my story for those with ears to hear. I hope to help others disentangle from these theories that have clouded our minds, robbed us of our spirituality and retarded the progress of nations. Humanity is going through a period of great turmoil and upheaval at this time, a lot is being revealed. Psycho-spiritual warfare is the new normal, learning to disbelieve the claims of scientism sets us free from a great deal of anguish that its believers must endure.

Chapter 2

Physics, Power, Secrets

The key to understanding the conspiracy behind physics is to realise that it's all about **power** and **secrets**. Physics is very much the science of power, it is the study of the secrets of 'matter' (earth + water) and 'energy' (fire + air).

If there are two things that governments love, it's power and secrets. Actually they happen to be in the business of acquiring as much of both as they possibly can. They acquire matter in the form of land, property, human resource, minerals, precious metals etc, and they acquire power in the form of knowledge or secrets. How many times have we heard it said *'knowledge is power'*?

The term "conspiracy theorist" was created by the CIA as a smear to dehumanise independent people who conduct research and investigate truth. But before I found myself tarred by this brush, I was a 'theorist' anyway, since beginning my academic journey in physics back in 1996. I have always done research and sought out the mysterious and unexplained in an effort to gain understanding, though for many years my attention was focused on fundamental physics and mathematics, the events of September 2001 opened my mind to the much larger playing field of international conspiracies.

As a physics theorist, I eventually got bored of thinking exclusively about atoms, gravity, and black holes, and curiosity compelled me to research other things, like music, history, alchemy, religion, or the plans and activities of human groups. After all, the only reason we know anything is because groups of people got together and conspired. People make plans, sometimes openly, sometimes secretly, sometimes for good, sometimes for evil, but humans conspiring is the only reason anything happens at all. To ignore conspiracies is to ignore the causes of things, to bury our heads in the sand.

But of course, conspiracy research is not welcome in the halls of academic physics, or any establishment institution for that matter. If you even joked about the moon landing, you'd be stripped of your titles and shown the door. It's a touchy subject, a real can of worms because the whole field of physics is itself a hotbed of lies, fallacies, occultism, conspiracies, and psychological operations.

The first thing I remember learning about physics was that it was **hard**, complicated as hell, only for the smartest people. Before I even went to university I heard that *quantum physics and relativity are the most advanced mental disciplines in the history of humanity, the stuff of genius, totally revolutionised our scientific understanding of the universe and gave birth to the wonders of the 20th century,* and so as a young boy this really appealed to me, it presented a challenge that I enthusiastically accepted.

I started my degree at St Andrews university studying a*strophysics*, but after two years I switched to *theoretical,* which covered most of the *astro* curriculum as well as lots of *quantum.* I learned everything I could about these subjects, took every class on quantum mechanics and field theory, immersed myself in dusty old text books into the wee hours of the night. I was one of the privileged six people to take the masters-year-only class on *general relativity,* Einstein's renowned magnum opus, I really fancied myself as a physics professor one day.

Being such a super complicated subject that utilises all the most advanced mathematics, there was only one professor in the whole university who could teach it, and truly I tell you, he spent the entire time with his head down reading from the text book. Didn't seem to have much of an intuition for it. Nevertheless I sat through all the lectures, fighting sleep and trying earnestly to comprehend everything that was being taught. I somehow managed to pass the 3-hour exam at the end of it all. I asked my professor why there weren't more people studying general relativity at the university and he said *'because it's hard and there isn't anything you can do with it'*.

I didn't realise this at the time, but in that one statement he pretty much summed up the whole of theoretical physics. It is hard, and there really isn't anything you can do with it. After the PhD, my head was so pickled with physics equations it took almost two decades to get some clarity and perspective on it. There's so much that just doesn't add up, but in the pressure of the academic track we just soak it in, pass the exam, and move onto the next thing.

20th Century Physics

Clearly there is a core of physics that is good, generally known as classical physics or natural philosophy, this includes: mechanics of moving objects, electricity and magnetism, optics, thermodynamics, waves and fields, vibration, music and so on. All of classical physics is fruitful. It is the scientific foundation of the industrial revolution and led directly to the modern technologies we enjoy today, from batteries and engines to computers, software and wireless communications. All machinery, engineering, and software is based on classical physics.

However, the 20th century and its two major wars brought with it a 'paradigm shift' in physics. The newfangled atomic theory of *'quantum mechanics'* and the newfangled gravitational theory of '*general relativity*' came to dominate the academic landscape, taking the centre stage in all higher education and television programming in relation to physics.

The boffins of the atomic age were held as high and mighty men of renown for their contributions. Huge sums of money got funnelled in that direction and Nobel prizes were handed out like candy to anyone who advanced the quantum agenda. Increasingly, physics became a subject associated with sci-fi and the most far-out ideas, wild claims, kooky thought-experiments, and complex equations calculating trivial nugatory.

The stated goal of this new physics was the unification of quantum and relativistic theories, which they say are totally incompatible with each other, but nevertheless when combined will lead us to a complete understanding of all things, the Grand Unified Theory (GUT).

As a gullible young student keen to make a difference in the world, I threw myself whole-heartedly into this new physics, believing all the hype and 'trusting the science', busting my brain every day to solve diabolically complicated equations and consume ever more spurious knowledge. But in the end I had to admit to myself; it was going nowhere, none of it really mattered, nobody actually cares. It doesn't help anyone.

In the years since graduating, I have thoroughly dismantled the many layers of modern physics and found it to be an occult conspiracy of monumental proportions, a deliberate effort to misinform and disempower the public, keeping us dependent on centralised systems of control.

Empowered individuals mean less need for government, and so government protects itself by disempowering the individual.

Manufacturing Dependency

In general, anything that empowers the individual is put under strict controls, whether it be through secrecy, price fixing or illegality. Statists can't have the masses getting their grubby hands on powerful knowledge. Imagine, for example, a scenario where an independent scientist discovers a new type of weapon, or limitless free energy, or the cure for all disease, or the secret of making gold. Do you think any government would sit idly by and let a private individual acquire all that power and share it with the world? Of course not. History has shown time and again that governments will go to great lengths to prevent, destroy, steal and/or conceal such work, and assassinate/ruin/slander/cancel/imprison the people behind it.

So while they require some degree of intelligence from citizens, to pass the exams, operate the machines and so on, they don't want people being too curious, and they certainly don't want people learning any knowledge that could undermine their power. They need you to be obedient, predictable human livestock. You must be either on the right or the left, with the reds or the blues, one of the sheep, or one of the goats. If you don't fit into the prescribed categories you're an 'extremist,' an 'outlier'. It's operated like a human farm because government is in the business of mind control and population management.

As individuals, we must learn to govern ourselves or we will *be governed*. Politicians polarise the populous. Even if you ignore them they will doggedly press ahead with policies that tear families and communities apart. No expense is spared in keeping us divided and fighting each other, clueless of the real issues, glued to our screens and hopelessly hooked on the narrative.

Though I am not opposed to government and higher education in principle, it appears the system we have in the west currently is totally compromised, unfit for purpose, it has sold its soul to the devil. Universities are centres of Marxist ideology, where young people are saddled with huge amounts debt before even starting their careers, a condition that greatly reduces the likelihood of them ever wanting to have children. It is a massive usury scam that slows population growth and harms the progress of nations by conditioning the youth with mind-numbing propaganda, leaving them unskilled and uninformed on real issues. In the age of the internet, it is preposterous to pay 50 grand a year to attend some lectures. You could buy a house or a large patch of land for the price of an undergraduate degree!

The Talking Dead

A corporation is a corp-oration which means *corpse talking*. Corporations are non-living entities, a legal fiction, we might even call them *demonic*, as it is only by way of their flesh-and-blood hosts (corporate employees) that they can talk in the world. If every employee quit their job at once, a corporation would have no voice, no living parts, and thus it would be unable to act in the world.

Being a non-living entity, corporations don't have the same morality or concern for life as we do. Their only concern is profit because it is by profit that they can tempt more men and women to give up their souls and serve the corporation. A good word for this is **egregore**, which is defined as '*a non-physical entity or thought-form that arises from the collective thoughts and emotions of a distinct group of individuals*'.

A corporation may arise from a common need, but what happens when that need is gone? It fights for survival, it borrows from the bank, it seeks investment, but that comes with strings (see DEI, ESG, etc). The political theatre of our time panders to these giant corporate egregores. Politicians bring no end of shame and embarrassment to the nations they are supposed to represent, as each new minister is more compromised than the last, the worst of the worst.

All western governments have become duplicitous, they are 'double agents' serving corporate masters who work to destroy the sovereignty and individuality of their host nations and usher in a new world order. Specifically, they are carrying out the directives of the so-called Kalergi plan[1], to the letter.

To understand this, we must realise that the UK, USA, EU, and UN that we hear so much about in the news are *not nations*, they are *corporations*, and they are controlled by international stakeholders who couldn't care less about us. In general, anything with 'united' or 'union' in the title, is a Roman Catholic corporation (such as my local football team Dundee United, which to my surprise was founded by catholic priests). As the saying goes 'all roads lead to Rome'.

However, this doesn't mean we can just point the finger at the Pope, it's not that simple, you see. The Holy See, a.k.a the See of Rome, which is the jurisdiction of the Pope, has been borrowing money from the Rothschild banking family for over 200 years. In fact, the Rothschild family, who also formed the state of Israel, have controlled the Vatican and the British Crown since the early 1800s, as well as almost every national and central bank in the realm.

Their tentacles reach deep into the pockets of every government and religious institution, which is why we see such unilateral agreement in the agendas of corporate entities. Essentially they all work for the 'iron bank'. We are living in a *debt-based society,* even the crown is in debt. This is symbolised by the sunken peak on the physical crown itself, showing that the institution is *weighed down* in debt.

Return of the King

In 2020, I learned of a man named Joseph Gregory Hallet, a.k.a King John III, who claims to be the rightful heir to the throne of England. The great (x10) grandson of Sir Walter Raleigh, and known colloquially as 'the hidden king', he has painstakingly exposed the true history of the illegitimate 'flat lie royals' in dozens of books over the last

[1] 11-Point Plan to Subvert the West by Richard Coudenhove-Kalergi

25 years[1]. Because of this, he also happens to be one of the most targeted, cancelled, and censored men in history, he has survived 18 assassination attempts and fulfilled a ton of biblical prophecies, but you've probably never heard of him.

Hallet is an accomplished historian and truther, and he has been quietly ascending toward the throne for many years. In his works he has provided masses of evidence that the British royal family are illegitimate and criminal, and have been breeding with the Rothschilds since the early 1800s. Our monarchs have no real sovereignty, they can never say anything wise or inspiring to the people. They can never lead, they just miserably recite the same old globalist rhetoric, and take as much as they can in tax. The use of body doubles is standard practice in royal circles, and Hallet claims there have been as many as 7 or 8 different versions of 'Charles' over the years. We must realise that 'the crown' as we've known it is largely a *facade*. We can almost think of these royal figures as characters in a TV soap opera, they are all disgraced in scandals and occasionally have to be replaced with new actors.

The King of England is supposed to be the protestant equivalent of the Pope, the 'defender of the faith', but currently there appears to be no such defence in the UK. Both catholicism and protestantism, which is the bulk of christendom in the west, are heavily indebted to a single Jewish banking family. The fact that our religious and royal institutions are so indebted to the bank, means that we the taxpayer suffers increasing austerity and hardship, while the politicians always find more money for war and foreign aid (a.k.a. depopulation and money laundering).

As a 'UK citizen' I've never known any different. The government is *constantly* funding foreign wars in our name, and importing the 3rd world while lying to the people about everything. That is just the nature of the beast. We've gotten so used to unelected bureaucrats, the idea of a legitimate ruler seems like a pure fairytale.

---

[1] Kingof.uk, 13 Book Series by Joseph Gregory Hallet a.k.a King John III

There are however some major shifts happening at the highest levels of power. History has been unfolding rapidly as I write this book. As of March 2024, Jacob Rothschild has died and most of the British royal family are either dead, sick, embroiled in scandal, or mysteriously missing. The pope is in hospital with the dreaded 'flu-like symptoms'. Princess Kate, the future queen of England, hasn't been seen for three months. Various establishment stalwarts have been dropping like flies, and it seems conditions are ripe for the emergence of a new power in the months and years ahead. With Gregory Hallet we may well have a true divinely appointed king ready to step up and take the reigns, time will tell.

Chapter 3

Counter-intelligence; Poisoning the Well

When you spend your whole life seeking truth and cultivating the quality of intelligence, it comes as a bit of a shock to learn that your own government invests huge amounts of time, effort, and money into misinforming citizens with lies, false history, and bad science, poisoning the well of public knowledge. This practice is known as **counter-intelligence**, and it is ground-zero for conspiracies and lies of all sorts, a mirky world where military secret services meet mass media, and politics meets occultism.

As an individual seeker, it is crucial to be aware of the existence and pervasive effect of counter-intelligence. It is a menace to civil society and the mortal enemy of true intelligence.

In governmental structure, 'intelligence' means *data gathering*, or more commonly known as *spying*, whereas 'counter-intelligence' means *any and all efforts taken to counter the spying operations of the enemy*. In general, this involves creating distractions, decoys, and disinformation to throw the enemy spies off the mark. But this operates on both a foreign and domestic level, so that means any curious seeker who loves his country is effectively treated by the government as a domestic threat (this is why the media always hates 'patriots').

In the UK, there is MI5 which runs domestic counter-intelligence, and MI6 for international. These 'intelligence services' report to the 'home secretary' and 'foreign secretary' respectively, who report to the PM, who reports to the crown. Domestic counter-intelligence consists largely of disinformation campaigns designed to distract, dumb-down and pacify the populous. It's all about mind control, fake news, propaganda, soap operas, spin etc, managing people's perceptions. There are no limits to their means of operation, they operate inside private companies and government departments as well as in education and the public arena[1].

The crown spends untold millions combatting the spread of truth online, funding controlled opposition agents, troll farms, and shills to sway public opinion. This is the Orwellian reality we find ourselves in, a condition known as 'fifth generation warfare' (5GW). The mind is a battleground where influencers wielding ideologies compete for the gold of your soul, and the powers-that-be are so deeply corrupt, they care more about silencing dissent than anything else.

When a government is illegitimate and engaged in criminal activity, they are fundamentally no different from gangs. They have no moral authority, no care for the common man. They may wear fancy suits and talk all posh-like but they frequently engage in such crimes that if the people knew even half the truth, they would rise up and make a change.

People will always seek out truth and justice unless they can be distracted, diverted, discouraged, dumbed down or bought-out in some way, so domestic counter-intelligence is big business. It's where most of the public

[1] New Zealand: a Blackmailers Guide, by Joseph Gregory Hallet

money goes. It's the damn that holds back the mob from waking up.

Inverted World

The official timeline of world events that we've been fed over the last 80 years or so is a false history that has been spun into the collective consciousness through the tell-lie-vision and the schools and universities. The internet has for a long time given us the means of understanding the lies and proving all of this. The people who figured it out first are brandished as 'conspiracy theorists' and attacked relentlessly by an army of legacy media puppets and controlled influencer shills.

The culture of governmental politics is fuelled by lies. It's all about hiding the truth, and this creates an 'inverted world' where truth is feared and considered as 'hate speech'. Politicians are paid to lie, as are the media talking heads, actors, and all the major voices and influencers, they are *lips for sale*, they will say (or suck) *anything* that their pay masters require, and you can be sure that the more influence they have, the more deeply compromised they are. A person of integrity and commitment to truth is a liability to a corrupt organisation, they don't want you. They need people who will bend, people who they can use to do the corporate dirty work, and modern hiring practices have been designed to reflect this.

Political power games are all motivated around shame and blackmail. Great power brings great temptation, and most worldly people will succumb to it, having not learned to control their lower animal nature. Intelligence services use 'honey traps' to seduce and ensnare influential people into compromising situations, which they then use as blackmail to control them from the shadows. The most well known example being Epstein Island, where a great many rich and famous people went to indulge themselves, and who are now at the mercy of the Israeli secret intelligence services who hold the video tapes. This of course gives Israel more power to steer and influence the nations in which these celebrities operate, as they will say or do *anything* to avoid being exposed. It's diabolical, but it works.

With all this corruption and skullduggery, the most pressing issue for globalists is always 'misinformation', which is the truth they don't want you to know. The anti-truth of the establishment has become such a calamity that the most appropriate term for the type of rulership we have in the UK is not a monarchy or a democracy nor a republic. It is certainly not a meritocracy or even a technocracy, we have a **kakistocracy,** a government run by the   least qualified, least principled people in society. It really is *that* bad.

It is often said that anybody who wishes to be a politician should be automatically disqualified from becoming one. This is why. It is a profession that somehow attracts the most psychotic and corrupt elements of society. In general, only the very worst people get to the top position. They are not elected, they are *selected*, and there is nothing honourable about it.

The Matrix & The Cave

The veil of fabricated factoids and the scripted reports broadcast by news media, are essentially counter-intelligence propaganda. It's only real in the minds of its believers. This is what has been dubbed "the matrix" by the movie of the same name.

'The matrix is the world they pull over your eyes to blind you from the truth' ~Morpheus.

In the movie, the matrix is accessed through the phone line and communications networks, you have to 'plug in' to it. The matrix is an information technology system designed to keep living human beings in a state of perpetual sleep, not knowing reality. Thus, to "escape the matrix" is really just to see clearly. T   o unplug and observe the world as it is, with open eyes, unencumbered by conditioned beliefs and illusion. The Matrix is said to be a 'revelation of the method', a fiction that shows us the truth about how 'they' plan to enslave us.

The whole predicament of the matrix is captured perfectly in Plato's timeless allegory of the cave.

In the image, the shadows on the wall represent the propaganda, the news and films and documentaries projected on screens to give credence to the lies, the hooded men are the secret agents and bad actors who work to create the illusions. Some people are sat in darkness watching the shadows on the wall, believing it to be real life, but if they only stood up, climbed the wall and headed towards the light, they would realise the truth and be free.

Part of the domestic counter-intelligence effort is to temper peoples curiosity in regards to energy, power, freedom and the nature of reality. The word 'government' means 'to steer the mind', so it should be no surprise that they also steer the direction of research and control the public perception of science, hiding the knowledge that is most threatening to their power.

They always need to project a sense of power and superiority over the populous, like a proud lion needing to be feared and worshipped. This is achieved with 'spin', fake media stories and crass entertainment designed to manufacture consent for everything they do, giving the impression that they have super-advanced technologies or weaponry made with some newfangled science forces[1].

---

[1] See 'The News Benders' (BBC 1968).

Non-Kinetic Military Action

The fifth-generation warfare waged by duplicitous governments against their own citizens is an exercise in perception management. To make the ruling elite seem big, mighty and powerful, and make the common people feel small, dependent, and weak. It is not a war fought with bombs and bullets, rather 'non-kinetic military action', counter-intelligence. Messaging, imagery, movies, music, narratives etc. The manipulation of the air waves.

In the book of Ephesians, it states that the ruler of this world is the '*Prince of the Powers of the Air*'. Air is the element in alchemy that corresponds with the mind, intellect, thought, words and communication. The "powers of the air" are the powers of the mind, the 'air waves', the broad-casting systems, news media, entertainment, music, education, and weather manipulation. When people are broadcasting, they are said to be *ON AIR*.

So while the current information technologies may be new and advanced, the bible tells us that we are always subjugated by he who dominates the air waves. The world is ruled by mind controllers, and in the days before the internet, it was the TV, cinema, radio, books, magazines, newspapers, pamphlets, posters, etc. In the ancient Greek and Roman times it was the amphitheatre stage, bread and circuses, the gladiator games. Anywhere that can amplify one voice to reach many ears. Essentially, he who can cast his voice the loudest has the greatest influence over the people. Whoever has the biggest bullhorn gets the most attention. But then this begs the question, who controls the bullhorns?

The fact that media is controlled by a small few is not even a controversial conspiracy theory any more, it is widely known by all serious people. Perhaps less understood are the principles upon which mass media operates and the purpose for it existence.

The image titled 'diversion summary' is a clip from the infamous and controversial treatise 'Silent Weapons for Quiet Wars.' A document allegedly found in a photocopier by an employee of Boeing in 1986. It succinctly lays out a plan for world domination by controlling the public intelligence and maintaining an infantile level of consciousness.

```
48
                    DIVERSION SUMMARY

MEDIA:    Keep the adult public attention diverted
          away from the real social issues, and
          captivated by matters of no real importance.

SCHOOLS:  Keep the young public ignorant of real
          mathematics, real economics, real law,
          and real history.

ENTERTAINMENT: Keep the public entertainment below
               a sixth grade level.

WORK: Keep the public busy, busy, busy, with no
      time to think; back on the farm with the
      other animals.
```

In these few short lines of text, we get a glimpse into the mentality of the people who have been ruling over us all these years. Here we have a small group of men with no national allegiance, conspiring to prevent everyone else from learning true science and history. Arresting the spiritual and economic development of nations. Actively poisoning the wellspring of culture.

Physics, and indeed all the sciences, have been commandeered by counter-intelligence operatives and are used to control and misdirect the public on matters of power, healing, transformation, and the true nature of the realm we live in.

Chapter 4

Arbores Mentis, Trees of the Mind

Theories are perfectly understood by analogy with a tree. They are a tree of knowledge in the astral fields of the human mind. Like a tree, theories have trunks, branches, leaves, and roots, and some of them also produce *fruit.* Classical physics, alchemy, and music are excellent examples of fruitful theories that blossom all year round, the abundance of their application knows no limits. Not only do they offer some explanation for how the universe works, in terms of vibration, transmutation of elements, and creativity, but they provide specific rules, techniques, and recipes, which can be practiced and applied repeatedly by anybody to create quality goods that benefit civilisation (instruments, music, medicine, etc.)

Theories are proposed explanations for the causes of natural phenomena. They do not exist in nature, they are a linguistic, logical structure of the human mind. For a theory to be considered a successful description of nature, it must be testable and must correctly predict the outcomes of scientific experiments.

When outcomes can be reliably predicted, tools and technology can be built upon the theoretical foundation, leading to new products, services, and applications that improve the quality of human life. This is how it works when theories bear fruit.

The Alchemy of Fruit

Fruit is symbolic of the gifts of nature. It represents the perfected end result of slow and laborious work, the transmutation of bitter black soil into the sweet colourful waters of life, delivered in a package that is tailored for human consumption. Fruit is universally healthy and always the perfect size to fit the human hand. It is all positive, beautiful, tasty, and clean. It provides flavour, refreshment and nourishment. If it is uneaten, it falls to the Earth and nourishes the soil, delivering a seed and growing a new tree. Nothing bad comes from fruit, and nothing bad gets in to fruit. All the bad is transformed into yumminess and seeds for the next generation. It's all part of the eternal incorruptible alchemy of creation.

The growth process of a tree is the transmutation of the seed, no impurities from the soil can make it into the fruiting body. If even one tiny corpuscle of impurity got into the fruit, then there would be no fruit. Fruit is the outcome of an alchemical purification process.

The tree is a symbol of *all* life, an earthen vortex. This is why we have the Tree of Life, every living thing is like a tree. Scientific theories begin as a seed idea and they grow to be great structures in the human mind, splitting off into various 'branches' of thought. Some trees grow very fast, tower over all the others, but produce no fruit. Though people may find some comfort in them, for shelter, or climbing, making themselves 'higher up' than everyone else, it is nevertheless a fruitless tree that is blocking the sunlight and restricting the growth down below.

Such trees can be easily blown over by strong wind, since their rapid ascension leaves them with brittle trunks and shallow roots. This is the condition of the theories taught in the world today, they stand like towers of intellectual architecture, held up as pinnacles of ingenuity, but they produce no fruits for humanity and rest on brittle assumptions that crumble when subjected to any kind of rigorous questioning or criticism.

Science vs Sophistry

As the saying goes, '*repetition is the mother of invention*', and just as the musician only produces music after repeated practice and effort, so theories only produces fruit when tested repeatedly and shown to be accurate and reliable. So when considering the whole body of scientific knowledge in general, we have to primarily differentiate it on this basis,

1. The science you can do (it produces a thing).

2. The science you must believe (it produces no thing).

The first type is all good, it's practical, verifiable, utilises the scientific method, it's empowering for all of humanity, it has its roots in alchemy and natural philosophy, and it produces a great many wonderful fruits. We gain skill and wisdom from working with it.

The second type does not use the scientific method, at least not properly, and nothing is produced with it. You can't test it for yourself, you can't build anything with it, but because of public schooling and relentless counter-intelligence in the popular culture, you simply *must* believe it. This is the air-bending art of **sophistry**, a type of speech and logical persuasion that is designed to sound plausible and convincing but is nevertheless misleading and deceptive. It confines itself to the explanatory layer of science, a region beyond sensing or testing.

Using sophistry, the potential power of true practical knowledge is tempered by the state with false explanations and nonsensical theories that we are conditioned to believe from a very young age, stuff that is so abstract we can't apply it to anything productive.

Sophists lack humility and the love of wisdom that motivates philosophers, they sneer at alchemy from behind their titles and jargon, seeking only status and wealth. Sophistry is pure AIR, words and spells, conditioning the mental landscape of the student, planting *Arbores Mentis (trees of the mind)*, convoluted networks of logic and reason, phoney explanations rooted in unsubstantiated beliefs, unrelated to physical or spiritual reality.

Coming to the Senses

As the caretaker of our own consciousness, it is crucial to root out these arboreal abominations from our mind, like weeding the garden, and cleaning the air of our body temple. Doing so provides clarity and objectivity, and for perhaps the first time in our lives, we truly come to the senses.

A characteristic of sophistry is that it always asks us to reject the evidence of our senses, to instead trust the experts and accept the existence of things not seen. The senses are the interface between our inner and outer worlds, and while they have limits, they are also far more acute than we give them credit for, we must learn to trust them.

Elementally, the senses are the gates to the soul. When a statement is true we say it 'makes sense', as though it is something we are constructing with each new piece of truth we acquire. When something is false we call it 'non-sense'. Most of these sophists and false-light pharisees function as spiritual **gate-keepers**, guarding the way to liberation, preventing us from accessing certain powers within.

Scientism is the framework of beliefs and assumptions held as gospel by this elite class of gate-keepers, social engineers, and counter-intelligence agents, and **sophistry** is the type of rhetoric they use to install those ideas in the culture at large.

In the subsequent chapters of section one, we will be dismantling and debunking the specific theories of scientism in more granular detail. In section two we will see how the true science of alchemy is perfectly congruent with the human senses, and does not require blind belief in any hypothetical particles, theories, or experts.

Chapter 5

The Five Elements of Scientism

Scientism is a patchwork of interrelated theories. It is referred to as 'secular' or 'humanist', and it is a belief system that places man at the apex of the cosmic hierarchy, particularly academic men with lots of titles and funny hats. It is a structure of synthetic language built up over many generations from a carefully chosen selection of theories and experiments. If theories are mental trees then scientism is a *psycho-spiritual jungle*, one in which many people are lost.

When looking at the history and chronology of scientific ideas, we can understand it more clearly by analogy with a tower; since it establishes a hierarchy of idols and achievements based on a timeline of landmark discoveries that constitute its core identity. Like a religion, it has its hierophants; those who wave their hands from the altar and profess complexities to the laypeople, and sycophants; those eager believers who feast on the fantastic and snarl at anyone who dares to question or criticise.

The roots of scientism reach deep into the psyche of the common people, informing many of our core beliefs and assumptions about the nature of reality, whether we understand the theory or not. Scientism affects us all. Even among self-proclaimed christians of various denominations, scientism dogma is widely accepted as fact, despite being completely at odds with the most rudimentary teachings of the bible. Many people are part way between worldliness and truth, and so they are still beholden to some 'beliefs of theoretical origin' that others have long since debunked.

There are five main belief systems that form the foundation of all modern scientism. Beware now, these are sacred cows that must never be questioned or criticised in 'the inverted world', you will be deemed a fool, alienated by your family, kicked out of your job, and uninvited from social activities for even talking about this stuff. *You have been warned!!*

OK, let's continue. The five elemental theories that comprise the worldview of scientism are:

1. Atomism (atomic, nuclear, quantum, particle physics);

2. Gravity (Newton, Einstein, Hawking);

3. Heliocentrism (Copernicus, Galileo, Kepler);

4. Evolution (Darwin, 'from goo to you by way of the zoo');

5. Germ Theory (Pasteur, Rockefeller, 'germs cause disease').

The numbering used in this list is not arbitrary. It represents the order of thought and the chronology of their ideation.

These are levels of the tower, each theory is built on the one before it, historically, mathematically and ideologically. One is only plausible if the one beneath is taken as fact.

These theories have been pummelled into the brains of the western populous as the de-facto scientific explanations for everything. We're expected to operate in the world as if they are reality, all agreed upon by an infallible consensus long ago, proven beyond any shadow of a doubt, assumed true by doctors and politicians and all reasonable men of society.

But in fact, none of it makes any sense or stands up to scientific scrutiny. These theories are believed not because they make sense, but because they are installed in our mind, propped up by reams of public money, research grants, books, television shows, news and movie propaganda. They are a collective hallucination reinforced by false imagery, sophistry, and counter-intelligence.

Many people have spent their whole lives believing in this stuff, and I am here to gently but firmly implore you, *don't be one of them.* A lot of money and hope and intellectual pride is invested in these beliefs, and a lot of immoral human activity is justified with them. Of course there are many more scientific theories when you get 'into the weeds.' We can't cover them all here, but you will find that all physical theories are rooted in these five, they are the *Five Elements of Scientism.*

From Babel to Babble

The Tower of Babel provides a potent symbol for the structure of scientism. It represents the consequences of unbridled human ambition, misguided effort, stubborn persistence in a monumental project which was always destined to failure. It represents fruitless human activity and the vain glorification of man; *look how great we are, we built a tower to heaven.* In reality the amount of effort required to build and sustain the tower would be increasingly costly, carrying one brick to the top could take an entire human life span. This is like the scientists of today who spend their whole lives putting one more brick on the tower, peddling babble and collecting all their awards and honours along the way. It's all glory to the man, but no benefits to the people on the ground.

In the image we see a set of scientific disciplines on the ground level, alchemy, music, shamanic healing, medicine, natural law, agriculture, engineering - these practices are rooted in *method,* and provide immeasurable benefit to mankind since the earliest known records. Scientism grows upward, into the mental realm of the high air, ever further away from the ground level of reality.

The tower consumes endless amounts of energy and life to sustain itself, but it produces nothing good. Just copious amounts of the most awful shit! The people on the ground are always dealing with the unholy sewage problem that comes down from the tower, every type of waste you can imagine. *Shit flows down, money flows up.*

The tower claims credit for everything, it is the unrestrained ego of mankind, *the greatest achievement ever.* It can be seen from every corner of earth, all must admire and serve the tower. It symbolises **transhumanism,** the efforts of man to transcend his earthly condition, to seek heaven prematurely, to break out of the top of the realm, or hack himself with technology to achieve a superhuman status.

Each layer of theory comes with a whole set of beliefs and claims. They are the pillars and archways holding up the next theory above it. It's notable also that each major theory comes with its own 'bogeyman'. From atomism we get the atom bomb. From gravity we get black holes. From heliocentrism we get aliens, and from evolution we get viruses, which are essentially *the bogeyman incarnate*, and the basis for the theories of vaccination, superbugs and ultimately COVID-19.

Whereas practical science deals with what is happening on the ground, the theoretical sciences just make stuff *up*, adding more and more layers to the tower at any and all expense. The higher the tower the more superior they feel to everyone else.

We must use razor sharp discernment and hard-nosed skepticism when looking at *any* scientific claims these days. We can't 'appeal to authority' or give anyone the benefit of the doubt. As we have learned throughout the 2020s, the consequences of unmerited trust in scientism can be devastating and even fatal.

In order to properly dismantle and rebuke this babbling colossus of pseudoscientific superstitions, it will take the next 6 chapters. I expect many will abandon the book at this point, cast it to the fire and curse me as a heretic, but for those willing to unlearn and dis-believe the non-science, there is a land of sweet milk and honey waiting for you in part two, an illumined paradise of empowering truth and practical science for the soul.

The remaining chapters of part one provide some fierce rebuttal and criticism to these *Five Elements of Scientism*. I will employ a combination of facts, logic and sarcasm, liberally mixed with anecdotes, informed opinion and a pinch of speculation. Please understand this is not meant to be an exhaustive treatise. We are dealing with a huge tower of thought spanning centuries, and it's really up to *you* to find your own way back to earth. But to begin the discourse we will start at the bottom work our way up.

Chapter 6

The Atomic Age Psy-op

Atomism is a school of thought that postulates all matter (all that matters) as consisting of infinitesimal, indivisible, corpuscular particles called Atoms. It is attributed to the Greek philosopher Democritus (460-370BC). It's not a new idea, although it became the commonly accepted scientific dogma over the course of the last few centuries. It currently masquerades under different names like 'quantum mechanics', 'nuclear physics', and 'particle physics' etc. It is a subject in which I was a bonafide expert at one point in life, but now, after having had 20 years to reflect on it, and with the benefit of a clarified mind detached from academic pride and ambition, I must confess that I find the whole field to be *highly* questionable.

The model of the atom we are taught at school, the one with the "electrons" orbiting a "nucleus" made of "neutrons" and "protons", is absolutely not a fact of reality.

Electrons, protons, neutrons are all **conjecture**, they are invented in the human mind and given as technical explanations for the elemental phenomena of fire, air, earth and water.

Quantum particles are mathematical in nature, they do not exist outside of the imaginal realm of concepts and ideals. They are not part of creation, they are not things in nature. They are hypothetical, unobservable and cannot be isolated or used to build anything.

To clarify, earthen materials do break down into grains of varying shapes and sizes which can be viewed under a microscope (like salt cubes and sand), and there are repeating geometric harmonic structures in crystals which give them their colour and form, interacting with specific wavelengths of light. But the power contained in the substance is diminished at smaller and smaller scales. When it comes to matter, *less is actually less*.

Atomists however will contend that somehow the power gets greater as we venture into the tiniest of tiny realms. Beyond the micro and nano and into the pico-, femto- and atto-meter scale of reality, there is an untapped source of world-destroying power locked up in the centre of the most infinitesimal corpuscular units.

Under the guise of an enlightened new perspective, atomism has subverted scientific thought over the last few centuries, normalising the belief that 'everything is made from atoms'. By the 19th century it incorporated with Darwinism into the belief that 'everything is made *by* atoms'. In this worldview, the Atom has replaced the Adam as the origin of man, and has replaced God as the creator of all things. As such, it became the focal point of all physical, metaphysical, and political power in the 20th century. It changed how we view the universe and even how we view our selves. In this brave new world of the atomic age, we're all just a bunch of atoms bumbling around in space.

Nobody has ever really seen an atom though, as they're way way beyond the range of senses, and there is this deep philosophical problem about the impossibility of effective observation at the quantum level ('the observation paradox'). Nevertheless we're told that atoms hold massive amounts of 'nuclear energy' concentrated in their centre, as well as the ability to self-organise into molecules and complex lifeforms, giving rise to all known life, the human race, and the entire universe as we know it without any need of an intelligent creator. The atomists have endowed the atom with the attributes of the divine, like a pagan idol, a humanist icon, an abstract mental concept to replace God, allowing the believer to discard any fears about judgement or morality.

The ancient Greek atomists were known for being extreme hedonists, abandoning decency and traditional moral principles in the pursuit of pleasure and power. It has been argued[1] that they invented atomism as a philosophy to justify selfish, hedonistic lifestyles, free from any worries of karma or judgement. After all, if everything is just atoms floating around in space, then the only source of goodness is *the bumping of atoms*. Atomism is fundamentally nihilistic and justifies all kinds of debauchery, materialism, and hyper-individualism.

Theories of the atom have changed many times over the last few thousand years, in the 20th century alone they've gotten ever more elaborate, ethereal, and mathematically complex to the point that few people can even pretend to know what they're supposed to be anymore.

Prior to the 20th century atoms were believed to be 100% solid stuff, indivisible by definition, impenetrably hard balls of pure matter. Then they claimed to split the atom, so now it's no longer an indivisible thing, it's a cosy little arrangement of different flavours of particles all spinning around each other like a mini solar system. Then after that they began saying atoms consist of 99.99999% empty space!

Extrapolating this historical trend in atomic physics research, we can expect that soon someone will discover the truth that atoms are **100% empty space** (and they'll get a Nobel prize for it).

[1] https://plato.stanford.edu/entries/atomism-ancient/

The Atomic Age

Atoms are so special and important to the government, that they have been given their own entire age. The so-called Atomic Age started with a bang in 1945, when the US bombed Hiroshima and Nagasaki, marking the end of WW2 and the start of a new post-war era. This was almost 2500 years after Democritus first came up with the idea of atoms (he was way ahead of his time). If these bombings are so significant as to have ushered us into a new world age, then we have to ask, when, or how does this age end?

Well, here's the kicker, it never ends! Technically, as long as knowledge of nuclear exists, we will be in the Atomic Age, so you'd better get used to it. But we have to ask, what is really meant by 'nuclear'? Is 'nuclear energy' really a thing? Are we even sure that the atomic nucleus exists?

Now let's be clear about one thing, big bombs exist. Nobody is denying that. There is technically no limit to how large of a blast you can create if you ignite the right amount of chemicals together. This issue is not even a question about the existence of bombs, it's about the use of the words 'nuclear' and 'atomic', and whether they are truly necessary or justified.

If they had just named them BFB's (Big F*cking Bombs) then that would be fine, there would be no disagreement and I wouldn't need to be having this conversation, but calling them 'nuclear' or 'atomic' is where the skullduggery comes into it. Just because a fire cracker goes boom, does not imply anything nuclear or atomic, these words are invented adjectives that refer specifically to hypothetical particles dreamed up by physicists, and they are frequently used as hyperbole or puffery to make things sound more extraordinary, mystical, or powerful, like "quantum this" and "nuclear that". They are intellectual power-words that cast the impression of dominance and superiority, the illusion of advanced magical science knowledge. But the naked truth is that bomb-making, like rocketry, is not as advanced as people think, it's all just about blowing stuff up for no good reason.

Fuel Me Once

Nuclear fuel, as it is called, comes from a particular type of ore known as Pitchblende or Uraninite, a grey-black rock which contains a mixture of heavy metal components such as Lead, Uranium, Thorium, and Radium.

Uranium is extracted from the Pitchblende, enriched and refined through a series of processes before being used as fuel in a reactor. The fuel rods act like the element in a kettle, hot metal that boils the water to create steam to drive the turbines.

Charged Uranium is hot to the touch, it stores and releases heat. We are told that it heats the water by way of 'radioactive nuclear decay' or 'thermal neutrons', but in view of alchemy there is no reason to believe the heat is anything different than regular radiation, also known as **light** or **fire**. We don't need to invoke imaginary particles to explain Uranium.

When Uranium cools down it is said to be *spent*, it is moved to a facility where it is kept in large pools of water until it is separated for Plutonium extraction. Plutonium is an entirely man made substance, a product of the transmutation of Uranium in the reactor, bits of it are laced throughout the spent fuel. Plutonium is extremely dense and volatile and makes for a potent explosive.

In the bombings of Hiroshima and Nagasaki, we are *told* the first bomb used Uranium fuel, and the second used Plutonium fuel, though it may have been just Napalm and Mustard gas[1]. Nobody is actually denying that these bombs were dropped, the bone of contention is the idea of "splitting the atom" and releasing "radioactive particles", it's the theory and propaganda behind the bomb.

Yes, Hiroshima and Nagasaki were burned to the ground, but it's crucial to realise that they suffered no 'nuclear fallout'. The local people built the cities back again right after the war, there's even a museum there now. If

[1] Michael Palmer - No Nukes But Mustard Gas and Napalm at Hiroshima and Nagasaki

nuclear radioactivity was real, then the whole region would be a post-apocalyptic wasteland for thousands of years.

The scorched shadows of people on the concrete is an effect caused by the very bright flash of radiation from the blast, it has nothing to do with atomic nuclei or quantum particles. Bright UV light bleaches concrete and creates shadows. Radiation can be dangerous, of course, due to its intensity or the frequencies within it, but that doesn't mean it is 'nuclear radioactivity'.

The so-called '**nuclear scare scam**' was first exposed in the 1970s and 80s by a man named Galen Winsor, a physicist who designed and operated many of the US government nuclear facilities, and was in charge of the national inventory of nuclear fuels. He talks of how they did all the Plutonium extraction by hand, with no shielding or protection, and all his staff loved their jobs, never suffering any ill effects from handling the "radioactive" material.

He claims to have frequently swam in the pools where the nuclear waste was kept, and to have drank a cup of water from it every day. The water has a blue glow said to be from "Cherenkov radiation". He even resorts to eating Uranium live on stage during his talks, to prove the point that it is not harmful.

Radiant Materials

So-called 'nuclear fuel' like this has been used in other applications such as submarines, and in the 1970s it was even used in pacemakers! Literally implanted right into the centre of the chest, a battery said to run for 88 years!

Though it may not be as dangerous as we're told, there clearly is power in these radiant materials. All metals have power, and Uranium and Plutonium represent the upper limits of metallic density. They are very similar in appearance to Lead, and are said to decay radioactively into

Lead. Being also fairly modern discoveries, it is fair to say that in alchemical language, Uranium can be thought of as a kind of 'heavy Lead', or 'radiant Lead'. They are found growing together in the same ore.

In alchemy, Lead corresponds to Saturn. It is considered the coagulated light of the planet manifested in creation. Curiously all the "radioactive" metals, Uranium, Plutonium, Thorium and Radium, are also named after pagan gods, Uranus, Pluto, Thor and Ra.

Thor corresponds with Jupiter, and Ra is the Sun. Gods and planets are sources of light, so as the planets radiate light, so do these metals, hence the naming convention.

Radium is a curious case worthy of a study all unto itself. It was heralded as a miracle of science for its ability to glow and provide sustained light and heat, it was put into all kinds of things including clothing, health & beauty products, toothpaste, and medicines, and sold on the open market during the first half of the 20th century. There are natural Radium pools located around the world which are said to have potent healing properties, and evidence suggesting that people used Radium to heat and power their homes.

All of this empowering healing technology was snuffed out by 'safety concerns', scare stories, and heavy handed government regulations as WW2 and the ensuing atomic age kicked off. By the 60s, based on a few scare stories (see the 'Radium girls' incident), Radium was no longer used in any consumer goods, and was effectively demonised and occulted, like Mercury, and other powerful substances.

When something becomes 'controlled' or illegal, that means it's for them and not for you. It's a power grab, a man-made law enforced by intimidation and hired thugs. Not a natural law, not God's law. It is designed in such a way that it is only ever applied 'downstream' by those with power against those without.

Resonance not Radioactivity

In physics we are taught that there are three types of radiation; Alpha, Beta and Gamma. Gamma radiation is just light, heat, fire, or what physics calls "photons", but Alpha and Beta are defined to be radioactive particles, solid spheres of physical matter ejected from a decaying body of substance.

It is this 'quantisation of radiation' that is the problem here. Atomists have to make everything into quantum particles. It would be more correct to think of Alpha and Beta as higher frequency radiation with a short range of action. Radiation is stronger when up close to the source. Alpha is close range, Beta is mid-range, Gamma is long range.

The click of the Geiger counter is not caused by the 'catching of an electron' or any such particle being spat out from the sample, the Geiger counter is clicking every time it receives radiation above a certain threshold of frequency. This is why it clicks more frantically closer to the source, because high frequency energy dampens quickly as you get further away from the source. It's all about frequency and resonance, there are no solid nuclear or atomic particles being spat out, and this is an important distinction to understand.

The ability of these materials to radiate light for long periods, is best understood by analogy to the Bell, which is able to radiate sound for a long time after it is struck. Radiant metals are a resonance effect, they absorb fiery energy and there is a sustain, decay and release of it over time, just like with sound.

Atomic Age, Nuclear Family

So who is responsible for starting this monstrous lie known as 'the atomic age'? Well, like so many great historical fibs, it all started with an American president.

In 1955, Dwight D. Eisenhower gave a speech that came to be known as 'Atoms for Peace', part of a government public relations exercise called 'Operation Candor'. In it, he set the tone for the cold war by the introduction of the "atomic dilemma", the idea that humanity could destroy itself at any moment with an atomic/nuclear blast. In the speech he said, '*To the making of these fateful decisions, the United States pledges before you, and therefore before the world, its determination to help solve the fearful atomic dilemma, to devote its entire heart and mind to find the way by which the miraculous inventiveness of man shall not be dedicated to his death, but consecrated to his life*'.

Until 1955, atomic research was highly secretive, but this put a message out to the whole world: *atoms are a thing, we've split them, and now we have the power to destroy the world.*

When you strip back the political rhetoric, what lies underneath is a thinly veiled threat of annihilation, '*I have a big f*cking bomb that could destroy your entire world, don't make me use it*'.

On an emotional level it doesn't matter one iota whether the bomb is made from some newfangled 'nukular' technology from the centre of the atom, all that matters is that it goes BOOM.

So this announcement paved the way for a new type of fear mongering, leading to such things as the "duck and cover" drills in American schools in the 1960s, where children were taught to duck under the desk in order to avoid getting vaporised by a Soviet nuke (not unlike making children wear face rags to protect themselves from a 'deadly virus').

The familiar black and white videos of houses getting incinerated by nuclear test explosions have all been debunked. They prove nothing, they are model houses, filmed in a movie studio for propaganda purposes. We must remember it was very easy for government to deceive the public in the early days of broadcasting, with everyone tuned in at the same time of night, high in their trust of public authorities. Big news stories were planned years in advance, it is a carefully constructed narrative.

Since Eisenhower set up this premise of the atomic age (with full support of the Brits), nuclear propaganda has been used to drive public fear and justify conflicts ever since. It does seem to be losing some effectiveness however, there are less facilities being built around the world, and the nuclear trend has been going out of fashion for decades. It can only be used to scare people for so long, there are so many new problems to deal with now, our brains are saturated, the threat of Soviet nuclear annihilation is brought up almost every week on the news. It's a tired old trope, way down near the bottom of my long list of concerns.

From where I stand, the real nuclear war is the war against the **nuclear family**, where mothers and fathers are made to work shitty jobs just to survive. Feminism and homosexuality are glorified, children are sent to government daycare centres to be programmed with scientism and fake history. This is one of the stated goals of the Kalergi plan, and once you see it you can't unsee it. Strong, resilient and self-sustaining families are a threat to government power. They work tirelessly to keep us divided, try to steal as much as they can in tax and make life as miserable as possible for everyone except their most loyal lapdogs.

Families are the nuclei of culture, and the government works to split them up and extract the energy therein. This is the real nuclear war. Since the start of the 'atomic age' we have seen a steady decline in family values and the sanctity of the *alchemical marriage*. Our duplicitous government has been instrumental in ensuring it happens at the policy level, it's no accident.

Intellectual Poaching

Atomists have tried to claim credit for various modern technologies, not just radiant materials and BFB's, but also such things as the laser and even the cathode-ray tube in the old television sets. But these are entirely products of classical physics and engineering, and can be explained perfectly well without invoking quantum lingo.

Cathode rays and so-called 'electron microscopes' use copper coils to generate heat and light, which is directed through a hole and then is deflected by an array of electromagnets to focus and modulate it. It's not a beam of 'electrons', but a beam of *light*, focused fire (yes, fire can be steered and focused with magnets *as well as* lenses). The term 'electron' is used to impose atomistic thinking over electricity, but electricity is pure elemental fire. It is *not* a stream of particles called 'electrons', those are conjecture.

LASER is said to be an acronym of 'light amplification by the stimulation of emission radiation', which sounds very technical and quantum. But in reality lasers are flashlights made with mirrors, filters and lenses to focus the light into a coherent monochromatic beam. There's nothing quantum about it. There's no photons bouncing around inside the device because photons are conjecture. It uses continuous or pulse-modulated light waves.

Another example of intellectual poaching is the so-called NMR or "Nuclear Magnetic Resonance" machines, those imaging devices used in hospitals to scan the brain. Often heralded as a modern application of nuclear physics. You may know them as MRI machines, which stands for Magnetic Resonance Imaging.

Why was the all-powerful N-word dropped from the acronym? Well, it's partly because nobody wants to put their head in a 'nuclear' machine, and the fact is there's actually nothing 'nuclear' about it anyway. The tech is entirely an application of electromagnetic engineering, no nuclear physicists were used in the making of it, and none are needed in the operation of it.

The great promise of quantum mechanics is the elusive 'quantum computer' which is alleged to be able to solve all mathematical codes instantaneously and at the same time! But just like with the manufactured 'nuclear arms race' and 'space race', there is now an alleged race on to build the first quantum computer. Whichever nation wins will have the ability to crack all encryptions in the world, to know every secret, and steal everyones money and passwords with a single press of the return key!

Seriously though, I have been following the quantum computing narrative since *1996*, and truly I tell you, it is pure smoke and mirrors, a lot of hype and jargon around a magical box that does nothing. If it were real, it would be the slowest field of technology research in all of human history. The theory doesn't even make any sense and the public presentations of quantum computing have been laughable, an insult to intelligence.

The first model was a black box, a refrigerator basically, it even had dry ice smoke coming out of it for that extra mystical effect. The latest one looks like an Arabian lamp shade. It's ridiculous, pure hype that doesn't actually do anything. It's another secretive government high-tech atomic marvel that is dangled in our faces to keep us feeling scared and small, but it will never materialise into anything substantial because its all based on false principles.

Of course there are very powerful computers, nobody is denying that. With parallel processing you can build a computer as powerful as you can afford. But there are no "quantum" computers, just like there are no "nuclear" bombs. There's just computers, bombs, and bullshitters.

Final Thought

If there is still some doubt in your mind as to the truth about nuclear, consider this. I obtained a PhD in nuclear physics, with no background checks, no top secret military clearance. No NDA's. Nobody made me sign anything to promise I will not use my powers for evil and try to build a nuke or reveal secrets to foreign enemies.

In theory, I could have left university, went and got myself some Uranium on the dark web and built a nuclear bomb. Or, if I was more enterprising I could have sold secrets to the Russians or the Chinese! But no, there was never any danger of me being able to do anything with this impractical knowledge. And actually the physics departments are already filled with Russians, Chinese and every flavour of foreigner you can imagine, so the knowledge is clearly not any kind of risk to national security. They will teach nuclear theory to anyone who's willing to pay the price and swallow it (but you may be better off swallowing some Uranium instead!).

Quantum, nuclear and atomic physics is pure sophistry, and relatively unchallenged. But to go through every single quantum equation and thought experiment and debunk them one by one would be terribly long-winded and boring and is not the purpose of this book. It is not even really necessary to debunk all the math, since we can see clearly it has produced no applications or benefits for humanity. It debunks itself by it's lack of usefulness.

Regarding the activities of so-called 'particle accelerator' labs who claim to be 'searching for new particles' or 'opening portals to other dimensions,' and so on, it shall suffice to say that they are not doing what they say they are doing, and nothing good or useful for mankind has emerged from these high security facilities. The idea of building the largest, most energy hungry machine in the world, purely to search for 'the god particle', is ludicrous and ironic. Scientism is predicated on the rejection of divinity, yet is still looking for God in all the wrong places.

All the alleged applications of quantum, atomic, and nuclear physics are fraudulent, sinister and highly suspect, it appears to be a form of occult counter-intelligence designed to hide the knowledge of radiant materials, transmutation and free energy.

Radiant materials have their dangers, everything fiery has potential destructive power. Dealing with them requires the same level of respect as we would have dealing with flames or electricity. However the elites have decided that muggles are too savage to handle such materials, so they give us theoretical physics to keep our minds occupied.

Unfortunately though, quantum mechanics can't fix your car, can't pay the bills or keep you warm in winter, it can't protect you against tyranny or heal your children when they're sick. It has literally no application in any areas of life. Every time the word 'quantum' is used without irony or criticism, you are being manipulated. Any products, services or theories with 'quantum' in the name should signal a red flag in your mind. You are being lied to, there is nothing 'quantum' about any of it.

Chapter 7

Planet Earth: The Mother of All Conspiracies

I first heard of 'flat earth' around 1999, playing the Stephen Jackson Illuminati card game with some friends at university. The cards each represent human groups with different special interests, and on the card for 'Flat Earthers' it says "*People laugh, but flat earthers know something*".

Of course, my student friends and I all laughed at the idea of people who believe the earth is flat. How could they be so stuck in the past? I kinda dismissed it as a weird joke, and after that I didn't think about it again for many years. During 2015-2016 it popped up a number of times online, eventually by recommendation from a friend, so I decided to look and see what it actually is these people believe.

I expected it to be some weird cultish thing like scientology, but what I found was just solid, verifiable scientific research that calls into question many of the theories we are taught about our world. For the most part, there was no nonsense at all, just straight-shooting facts and hard questions that are thought provoking and irrefutable. As someone coming from a scientific background, I was well impressed by how meticulous and well-reasoned the flat earth research was, it was a breath of fresh air to see the scientific method being used so effectively. I couldn't understand why I hadn't learned *any* of this in university, it's really fundamental stuff. It took a few months of watching presentations, doing experiments and having many heated conversations with people, but eventually I came to a place of 100% *knowing* that our world is not a planet spinning through space. I may not know 100% what it is, but I know 100% what it is not, and it's not a spinning ball. The Illuminati cards were right, flat earthers do *know something*.

The process of conversion is a one-way street, nobody ever goes back to believing in the ball, there are no ex-flat-earthers as far as I know, because there is actually no reason to believe you are spinning once you know that you are not. But how does one get to a place of knowing such a thing?

Well, start by asking yourself, how do *you* know that you're on a spinning ball flying through space? You have to set about trying to prove the globe, something that seems like it should be quite an easy task (especially for a boffin such as myself) but it turns out is actually quite impossible.

Many will tell you the same story, becoming a flat earther is the result of having tried to prove the globe and failed. The irony is flat earthers are treated as the most stupid people in society, a proper fool in the negative sense, a symbol of weirdness and wrong-think, a group of people not even worth listening to. The globe is so entrenched in the collective consciousness, that it is generally deemed to be an unquestionable fact of reality.

To do the work it requires a position of neutrality, no attachment to any particular outcome, simply to look at all the evidence for and against the spinning ball earth. In doing this we have to be comfortable being the Fool. People will call us a fool for even talking about it. We must be open minded, curious, humble, and ready to have our worldview challenged.

Going in with a hard head and a zealous attachment to the globe will get you nowhere. Eventually, once the various proofs are understood, and the beliefs and assumptions of the globe model have been overcome from every conceivable angle, it all just clicks into place.

I remember vividly the day I realised I wasn't spinning through space, it was the most profound awakening of my life, a true enlightenment experience, a new dawn, finally getting 'out of the mind' and 'coming to the senses'. The globe earth is often called the **mother of all conspiracies**, and for good reason, it's a conspiracy about the nature of our mother, Earth! And when you internalise this it is like a master key that makes all other conspiracies very transparent and easy to spot.

The topic has been presented and debated very thoroughly for a long time now. There are literally hundreds of verifiable scientific experiments to consider[1] and some amazing resources and dedicated people[2] devoted to giving you all the best information on every question you might have.

In general, it is a topic best discussed by video presentation, since the globe is an image largely promulgated through the medium of video. However, if you really wish to try and prove the existence of the globe for yourself, let me save you some time, there are only two tests that really matter:

1) proof of spinning;

2) proof of curved horizon.

Here's the catch: you can't use images from NASA as your 'proof' because NASA has been shown to be a fraudulent organisation that lies to the world and fabricates fake imagery, many times over. Plus, it's unscientific and a

[1] 200 Proofs Earth Not a Spinning Ball, by Eric Dubay
[2] Flat Earth Sun, Moon & Zodiac app, by David Weiss (DITRH)

logical fallacy to 'appeal to authority'. You have to prove it using the scientific method, techniques that can be repeated by independent people. All NASA imagery is unverifiable and unfalsifiable, so it's useless as evidence for anything (the 'space program' will be covered in the next chapter).

When I set about trying to prove this back in 2016, I thought it would be child's play. With my trusty PhD and advanced mathematical skills, and since I was flying 'around the globe' in planes all the time, I could undoubtedly prove it, easily! But the more I looked and the harder I tried, I just couldn't. I searched for globe evidence every single day for 3-4 years. It was an obsession, I kept thinking maybe there was something I overlooked, some test that proves it. I soured many relationships due to broaching the subject, and I follow the debate closely, but I have never found a single reason to believe in the globe in all the years since. The case for the globe gets weaker with each passing year, while flat earthers grow in number constantly.

What's clear is that academics don't engage with it on a sincere level. They either completely ignore it, or use ad-hominem attacks to slander and belittle the researchers, as if the whole topic is beneath them. An insult to their intellect, a conversation not worth having. This is intellectual bypassing. They just block you and smear you and carry on as normal.

From 2015 through to 2018, a golden era for the free flow of information online, almost every single day I found more reasons to doubt the globe model of earth. And almost every time I tried to talk to someone about it, I was shutdown, dismissed as a fool.

I eventually opted to keep it out of social conversation. It's far too much of a thankless labour trying to re-educate people in cosmology during the short windows of time we have together, especially when most don't even want to learn. All the alchemy texts I was reading warned against trying to share higher knowledge with people who are not ready or willing for it. And I felt like there was no reason why anyone would believe me. In the eyes of the world I was a professional fool, not a serious scientist.

Nevertheless, I knew in my heart of hearts that the globe is a lie. I could find no real evidence for the existence of this giant spinning ball we call "planet earth", and all the theories it was based upon were crumbling under scrutiny. It became clear as day that the whole thing is very a clever fabrication.

Moving Earth Theory

It is sometimes said rhetorically that Nicolas Copernicus 'set the earth in motion' with his theory of the solar system in the 1500's. Known as the "Copernican Revolution", it marked the transition point from a stationary world to a revolving world.

But of course this is pure hyperbole. He did not set the earth in motion, that would be impossible, the earth is just the same now as it was before Copernicus, the only thing that changed was the beliefs of the Jesuit clergymen.

Earth didn't start spinning when Copernicus declared his theory, instead we are expected to believe that it was spinning the whole entire time and that the primitive peoples prior to the 15th century didn't notice they were spinning, they were so unevolved and lacking understanding of gravity that they naively believed the earth to be stationary. The messaging here is, *if you don't believe in Copernicus, you're a savage Neanderthal*, and this is exactly how people treat flat earthers, like they shouldn't even be allowed to exist anymore.

The Copernican theory became known as Heliocentrism and is essentially a modern revival of the worship of the Sun (Helios) as the central fire and life-giver of creation. Solar worship can seem reasonable at first glance, the Sun is indeed glorious and awesome after all. It does appear to be the main source of light and life, it deserves our respect and gratitude for sure. But

Heliocentrism is more than that. It claims that the entire human realm is spinning through space like a giant tennis ball, while simultaneously flying around the Sun at breakneck speed, magically bound to it by an invisible thread, sort of like a cosmic Swingball™.

Before this model was inserted into the Jesuit education curriculum in the 1800's, it was widely considered a heresy due to it's opposition to scripture and common sense, and it was known more appropriately as 'The Moving Earth Theory', or 'The Theory of Falling Bodies', since in space everything is supposed to be falling all the time.

But it's important to realise that all practical, fruitful fields of scientific work are based in a **geocentric** frame of reference, meaning that they don't account for the spinning globe ball in their work, there's no need. Whether it be chemistry, alchemy, architecture, engineering, agriculture, medicine, even aviation and navigation, they are all based in geocentric science.

All aircraft navigation software uses a 'flat non-rotating earth assumption' in calculations, and things like drones, helicopters and airships are able to hover in one spot because the ground is literally not spinning away beneath them.

Try asking a pilot about the flat earth, you may be surprised by his response. There are more pilots who know about it than any other profession. It's like an industry secret. Any pilot with knowledge of classical mechanics knows he could never land on a spinning ball, the forces involved would be far too extreme.

Airplanes generally fly in a straight line horizontally over a *plane* through the *Air* toward the *flat horizon*. It's written into the autopilot software. This is the mechanics of flight. Many flight paths have been shown to make no sense on a spherical map, but make perfect direct lines on a flat circular map (New Zealand to Argentina for example). There are also several emergency landing events that are a matter of public record, that clearly show flight paths consistent with a flat world map.

Another point which has been proven many times over with the help of modern camera technology (Nikon P900+), is that boats going out to sea don't disappear over the curve of the earth globe as we've been told, in fact they can be brought back into view with a decent zoom lens.

Due to perspective, boats get smaller the further away they are, and eventually disappear *as if* they are below the horizon, but in reality they are still on the same level as you, just at a distance which exceeds the angular resolution of the eyes.

The official rate of curvature of the globe is stated as '8 inches per mile squared', but this is just not observed with modern camera tech.

But Earth Isn't Actually Flat

The term 'flat earth' is problematic however. It creates a cognitive dissonance because it's not actually the Earth that is flat, **it's the water**. Earth is rough and lumpy and takes all kinds of shapes and forms, like mountains and valleys and trees and humans and so on. It can be flattened by force, but it's not flat by default. It is the ocean surface that is a level flat plane, like the surface of any fixed body of water.

It is not 'flat earth' but 'Planet Earth' that is the conspiracy. **Planet Earth does not exist.** It's an entirely fictional construct, like Pandora, Tatooine, or LV-426.

The word '*planet*' is from Greek *planetos* meaning 'wandering star'. It refers to the five star-like objects that *wander* in the night sky. Mercury, Venus, Mars, Jupiter, Saturn, are the wandering stars, the so-called 'planets'.

Earth is the dry land beneath our feet, the element that our bodies are made from, our tissues, teeth and bones.

We are the Earth, and our ground state is one of **stillness** and **rest**.

Earth is **not** a planet.

Earth is **not** a wandering star.

Earth is **not** where we are, it's *what we are*.

Earth is *flesh* and *bone.*

In section two of this book we will dive more deeply into the physical properties of the Earth element, but it's important to understand this distinction. The fictional globe planet was named after the element Earth, but the element Earth is itself nothing like a spinning ball flying through space.

Spinning is Acceleration

The Heliocentric spinning globe theory of the Jesuits, has been promulgated relentlessly in public education, of which they operate and control the majority, as well as science fiction books and movies, TV news narratives, and secretive government agencies like NASA and MI5. Most people accept it without question, but some have tried to prove it with hard science, those people are called 'flat earthers,' and they don't deserve to exist.

Funnily enough, most globes come with a sticker on the bottom explicitly stating '*not for educational purposes*'. Spinning at 1000mph, and orbiting the sun at 66000mph, as we're told, is a very extreme physical condition to be in. A state of constant acceleration and change of direction, there's all kinds of forces and effects that would be felt, none of which are found to be measurable in reality, nor accounted for in the mechanics of flight.

Would anybody believe they are spinning if it wasn't for being repeatedly told about it at school and on TV? It's really quite a humorous and peculiar state of affairs, that one man believes he is spinning, while the next man believes he is stationary. If we were always spinning then stillness would not exist, we wouldn't even be able to have this conversation. I'm sure there are people who would argue the point, but it is my sincere observation from all my years of life that **stillness exists**, it is an inherent property of the element of Earth.

Whereas Fire expands and rises up, Water condenses and flows down, and the Air whirls and blows, Earth is completely still. It is the manifestation of the principle of **inertia.** It resists movement, stillness is it's natural preferred state. Earth only moves when pushed or pulled (also known as Newton's first law).

The much touted Michelson-Morley experiment was designed to measure the alleged movement of the globe earth. It consists of light beams pointing in two perpendicular directions, one in the direction that 'planet earth' is allegedly moving, and the other at 90 degrees to it. They reasoned that light would move slower in the direction of movement due to 'Aether drag', but when they failed to observe this, they declared that it's because the Aether doesn't exist.

So even though they found no evidence earth was moving, they assumed it is and continued to believe that it is, and used the result to try and suppress knowledge of Aether instead. The experiment is a classic example of a *foregone conclusion.*

If earth was spinning, we would not be able to build anything, or carry out even basic tasks due to the forces at play. Anything that is on the outside of a ball is destined to get flung off once it starts spinning. Life on a spinning ball is impossi-ball.

We may be able to live on the *inside* of a spinning ball, since you can walk around on it to some degree (same principle as the hamster wheel), but attempting to walk on the *outside* of a ball that is spinning and orbiting on three different axes at thousands of miles an hour, would undoubtedly result in a severe flinging.

But Gravity Sucks

We're told that this is where gravity comes into play. Gravity supposedly provides a comfortable downward pull which is *just right* to hold the oceans and the people on the ground, while allowing birds and insects and airplanes to fly with ease. A magical force that creates the sensation of perfect stillness and warmth while we hurtle through the zero degree vacuum of outer space, spinning, orbiting and wobbling like a giant cosmic Waltzer.

The reason people get so upset when you question gravity, is because it is the lynchpin that holds their entire concept of reality together. It *must* be real, otherwise *nothing* could exist! Many people wrongly think gravity is some *thing* that has been discovered or proven, but it is not a thing, it is a *theory*, invented and fictitious, never proven but always assumed.

Gravity is *said to be* a weak attractive force emanating from the nucleus of every atom because of its mass. The problem with this idea is three-fold,

1) It's pure sophistry, a made-up equation;

2) It's too weak to be measured, but *just* strong enough to hold the scientism worldview together.

3) If we entertain the idea that it does exist, it leads to the inevitable conclusion that all matter (all that matters) will ultimately be sucked toward the area of greatest density and crushed under its own weight into oblivion ('black hole' or 'big crunch').

This is why people who entertain gravity end up obsessing over black holes, they are a limiting case in the made-up equation, but they are not observed in nature. Claims that black holes have been observed with telescopes in the centres of galaxies should be taken with a hefty pinch of geocentric salt, being as they are, based on stacks of highly questionable beliefs and assumptions about light, gravity and the sky.

Gravity is a contrived explanation for the effect of falling, hence its original name, the 'Theory of Falling Bodies'. The root of the word 'gravity' is *grave*, because this is where you end up. As a 'fallen being' yourself, the only way is *down*, dead in the ground with the rest of the atoms.

But the observed effect of the falling apple does not imply the existence of 'a force called gravity' as the cause. There is no need to explain the phenomena of falling by invoking a fictitious force. Density and buoyancy are sufficient principles to explain the rising and falling of objects, as well as electrostatic attraction and repulsion. It is a universal principle of alchemy that when a substance is more dense than its medium, it sinks down, when it is less dense than the medium, it rises up, this is the essence of distillation.

Gravity dictates that nothing can go up, everything must come down. Because it is contrived and not based on measurable reality, it is fruitless. It has not produced any technology or led to any benefits for mankind. To combat the blatant failures of the gravitational theory, physicists have postulated new forces that are alleged to compensate for gravity's destructive all-sucking effect, things such as "anti-gravity" or "dark matter", which are said to work *against* the attractive force to balance everything out again so it all feels perfectly calm and stationary like we observe.

This is fiction on top of fiction. They are attempting to compensate for the absurdity of the original idea by inventing even more absurd ideas. There are no such things as 'black holes', 'bendy space-time' or 'gravity', and anyone who tries to convince you otherwise is misleading you and wasting your time. Think of the symbolism of a 'black hole' - it is literally nothingness, and it sucks all your light/life. It's a total waste of time even thinking about them.

It is no exaggeration to say that these concepts are more at home in an episode of Star Trek or Futurama than they are in real life. They might make for fantastic story telling and epic 'Space Oprah', but don't get caught up in the sci-fi fantasy, they have no correspondence in the true, empirical reality of creation.

The original measure of gravity, which is alleged to have proved its existence, is called the Cavendish experiment (1797). It is a famously difficult experiment to conduct due to the extremely sensitive nature of the apparatus. Measurements are so tiny that almost anything could be causing the readings. It's a similar fallacy to the so-called LIGO gravitational wave detector; the sensitivity of the instrument is so incredibly precise that any minuscule blip on a graph can be blown out of all proportion and interpreted as evidence of a 'galactic gravity wave' or 'supernova collapse' or some such thing. These alleged 'proofs' are absolutely feeble.

Stationary and Enclosed

Perhaps the strongest argument in favour of a stationary enclosed realm, is the issue of air pressure. We live in a pressurised air environment, and it's fair to say that pressurised air requires containment. The Air with it's barometric pressure of 14.7 pounds per square inch, must be enclosed in a sealed container. When no air or water can get in or out, this is called *Hermetically Sealed.*

The globe model claims that the surface of 'planet earth' is wide open to the cold vacuum of space, but if this were the case, the atmosphere would get sucked off the planet instantly to equalise pressure with the surrounding vacuum (which is also an infinitely larger space). You can't have stable pressurised atmosphere that is not contained, gasses will always disperse into an area of low pressure. There are people who try to claim that 'gravity is the container'. That it somehow holds the gasses onto the outside of the planet in a 'gravity well' in spite of the **infinite vacuum** all around, this is pure desperation. The theoretical notion of the 'ionosphere' is also not sufficient to contain pressurised Air. It too would get sucked into space, like all the other 'spheres' in the so-called 'atmo-' sphere (atom-sphere?).

If we take a cross section of the realm as it appears to our senses, and in light of all that is scientifically verifiable and in alignment with the ancient teachings of many old world religions, we get a consistent view of creation as something more like a 'snow globe' or **terrarium**.

This is not unprecedented either since people have grown whole gardens inside of Hermetically sealed glass containers. There is the famous case of David Latimer (pictured), who planted his terrarium on Easter Sunday of 1960. Since then has only opened it once, in 1972, to put a little more water in. The garden is thriving to this day, and only requires sunlight.

In this view of the realm as an enclosed ecological system, it is sealed by a dome shaped barrier known as the **firmament**. The whole thing is stationary with respect to the Aether, frozen in Antarctic ice, **immovable**.

The firmament is defined in the bible, in Genesis 1:6 'And God said, Let there be a *firmament* in the midst of the waters, and let it divide the waters from the waters.' We don't often use the word *waters* in plural form like this. Some have suggested that it may be another term for *Aether*, the primary paternal substance of existence, the father of fire and mother of oceans.

Earth is the dry land that precipitates out of the great deep, a product of the Air and Fire acting on the Water. The Sun, Moon, and stars are focal points of light that move through the firmament in circular paths overhead, high above the earth and the ocean below. They are not objects, or lands to be conquered with flags and buggies, but rather they function like poles of a battery. The sun being positive, and the moon negative.

The ocean is flat and level, the great deep is basically 'the bottom half of the realm'. Water is the incompressible element, and it is capable of receiving all frequencies of light. It's surface is a great plane that marks the interface with the element of Air.

According to Genesis 1:1, the spirit of God originated in the surface of the waters. So God did not create the waters, *the waters created God.* God is said to have created light (fire) and the firmament (possibly a form of quartz), which set the boundaries of the realm and the space within which creation could take place.

In this conception of the cosmos, up is up and down is down, Heaven is above the sky and Hell below the ground. The vertical axis is absolute. Up and down are a measure of morality and alignment with God. This is why we say 'upstanding' and 'upright' are godly attributes, and why human beings are the only creatures to naturally walk upright and hold that vertical alignment, they are made in the divine image. God being the **most high**.

Discworld

Perhaps the author Terry Pratchett was giving us a clue with his *Discworld* series of books. It seems that the true map of our world is a **flat circular disc** (*both* flat *and* round), with the north pole in the centre. Known in map jargon as the 'azimuthal equidistant projection', it is found on Gleason's standard map of the world, used successfully for navigation for over a century. It is also found in the logo of the UN, the WHO, and several other international 'globalist' organisations.

UN (left) and WHO (right) logos with flat earth maps

I like to think of it as the view from Polaris. In this map, Australia is not 'down under' anymore, that's a globalist colloquialism, its now 'far out'. Australia is the long continent in the 1-2 o'clock position, and New Zealand is the islands just off the 12 o'clock position, which marks the 'international date line'.

Though there are potentially some scaling issues in this map at the extreme southern latitudes, it works very well for navigation and seems to be good enough for our psychotic unelected overlords to use as their emblem (and they have full access to the realm).

The grid lines over the map segment it into 33 zones, the middle circle is the Arctic circle (66.6 degrees north), and the outer circle is the Antarctic circle (66.6 degrees south[1]). Anything beyond that (represented by the Olive wreaths) is technically Antartica. So Antartica is not shown as a land on this map, nor is the north pole, which is apparently just a watery expanse at the centre of the world. Antartica is not an island at the bottom of the globe-ball, but rather it is the ice shelf surrounding the flat circular disc ocean in which the continents sit. Antartica is the outermost circumference of the realm, the edge of the puddle, as it were.

---

[1] Based on the 23.4 degree deviation between the ecliptic (path of the sun) and celestial equator. 90 - 23.4 = 66.6. In the globe model they call this is 'the axial tilt of planet earth,' or **obliquity**.

If we think of a clock face, north is inward toward the centre, south is outward toward the edge, east is anti-clockwise, west is clock-wise. The sun, moon, and planets move clockwise around the realm (east to west).

The Antarctic treaty of 1959 exists to prohibit any individuals from accessing that southern ring of icy wilderness beyond the 66th parallel. All nations agree to forbid any independent travel or exploration, you can only go to designated research facilities and receive the official tours, you can't go off exploring Antartica by yourself, it's 'out of bounds', you will be removed by military force.

I don't know what lies beyond the 66th parallel and I don't know who does. Some have claimed there is other land (see Admiral Byrd). Various sketchy looking maps have cropped up in recent years showing extra rings of oceans, islands, and continents beyond Antartica, but I take these with with a hefty pinch of salt since it's easy to make a fake map for a territory nobody has ever seen before. The idea of 'extra territory' is appealing since it implies we can still have 'extra-terrestrials' without the outer space nonsense, but I'm not sold on it. Until free travel is permitted in the north and south zones, we can only speculate how vast the plane might extend.

Occulting The Edges

Unlike the globe, the flat earth must have a perimeter. At some point there has to be a solid impenetrable wall where the realm ends. Like *The Truman Show*, the world conspires to prevent us from going there, it is hidden and blocked from us. The Antarctic treaty suggests that we are being 'penned in', if it was just a large icy island then there would be no need for all the security and defence. Our little world pond is surrounded 360 degrees by an international force of armed guards who won't let us see what's beyond. Why must it be this way?

The north pole has been removed from maps in recent decades, and though all magnetic field lines point toward it, and Auroras emanate from it, we are expected to believe there is nothing there but a cold empty ocean and lonely polar bears desperately seeking icebergs.

The Arctic and Antarctic circles have been occulted, not even allowed to be called lands, nations, or countries, they are hidden from public access. Whatever is there, 'they' don't want us knowing about it. Older maps based on scripture depict a sacred land (Hyperborea or Mount Meru) at the centre of the realm with four rivers flowing outward to fill the seas.

The 66th parallels, both north and south, mark the limits of the zones that muggles are allowed to travel in. Since the majority of travel is now done by airplane, people can only fly to designated locations on the map that have airports. With zeppelins or airships, Helium/Hydrogen or hot-air balloons, people can travel all over the plane and land anywhere, with no need of airports.

Airship would be the best method for exploring beyond the 66th parallels. Due to the Hindenburg disaster of 1937, this technology has been almost completely erased from our culture, only appearing occasionally for advertising purposes and gimmicks (the Goodyear blimp etc).

We are told that the explosion of the Hindenburg was a stark warning of the dangers of using Hydrogen gas to float balloons, and led to the phasing out of Airships in favour of Airplanes. But what's clear now, is that Airships can not only be used to go anywhere and explore the entire realm, but they also prove that the earth is a stationary plane without borders, and that gravity isn't a thing.

The Hindenburg was a false-flag operation, a psy-op to justify the forced obsolescence of this marvellous aetheric technology. You don't abolish an entire mode of transport worldwide due to one accident! It's like cancelling all boats because of the Titanic. The Hindenburg was also a far smaller disaster than the Titanic (36 dead allegedly).

Atoms in Outer Space

Heliocentrism and the globe theory go hand in hand, they are constructed from atomistic thinking and the theory of gravity. The model of the solar system and the model of the atom are nearly identical, even the most inattentive physics student notices this. The only real difference between the solar system and the atom is the scale of object being theorised; one is *unimaginably big*, the other *unimaginably small.*

The Sun corresponds with the nucleus as both are alleged to be sources of nuclear and gravitational power, and the planets are said to be like the electrons orbiting and spinning around it. Gravity is the magic sauce that binds it all together on the big scale, and 'the nuclear force' is what binds it together on the small scale. Astrophysics is the love child of heliocentrism and nuclear theory. Astrophysics is nuclear physics in outer space, a theory inside a theory.

A founding assumption of Astrophysics is that the Sun and stars are essentially giant nuclear reactors, constantly exploding with the force of a trillion Hiroshimas every second, all while spinning and going round and round in orbits while held perfectly in place by our trusty old friend gravity.

It must be noted that before these explanations were invented, the star canopy was universally known as the heavens. So Astrophysics has effectively placed itself between man and heaven, denying the divine by 'mansplaining' the heavens into such inscrutable mathematical oblivion that it's too boring for anyone to even care about.

Instead of heaven being the handiwork of God, it's now called "outer space." It is the professional domain of an elite group of physicists, a fantastical realm populated by aliens and astronauts, where anything is possible, but nothing ever happens, and everything is so big and far away you'll never get to see it in a million years.

Astrophysics should not be considered superior to Astrology or Astrotheology, which are both divinely inspired sciences and an immense source of wisdom, existing long before heliocentric and atomic ideology 'infected' the tree of knowledge.

Astrophysics is frequently employed in science fiction books, games, and movies to give some sense of credibility to the fantasy being spun. I was one of those who faithfully watched every episode of Star Trek like it was a manual for our future, and I actually understood all the science they were referring to in the episodes. I can tell you now though, it is all theories built on top of theories. Wild claims and speculation, jargon-porn, fuel for the fantasies of heliocentric believers.

Astrology has been rightly called "the science of sciences" or "the highest science", and although mainstreamers treat it with derision and skepticism, it is actually so incredibly accurate and useful that it puts astrophysics to shame. Astrophysics occults astrology, it literally teaches students to view astrology with sneering contempt. Astrophysics is not a path to wisdom, it is total junk science, founded entirely on unproven assumptions.

The word 'Astro' or 'Astr' means 'Star' or 'Light'. To the best of my knowledge nobody knows exactly what stars are, other than the fact they are **light**. We know they must be light because we can see them twinkle with our eyes, they are light *by definition.*

Outer space is not a place, it's a fictional concept beyond sensory comprehension, just like 'planet earth'. The empty vacuum of space corresponds to the emptiness of the physicists mind, the mental canvas upon which to perform thought experiments, the blackboard upon which the physics equations are written. The vacuum of space is just an idealised state of nothingness.

To deny outer space is not to deny the stars. Everyone sees the stars, they are an ever present mystery, a blanket of illumination, Gods handiwork. With the exception of the wandering stars (planets), every star has a fixed angular coordinate in the sky and moves in a circle around Polaris, which remains fixed above the north pole. This is has been repeatedly verified by time-lapse photography aimed at Polaris, and can be seen with sky mapping software such as *Stellarium.*

Any claims about the size of, or distance to the stars being millions of light years away, or equal in weight to a million solar masses, or any references to 'astronomical units' or 'parsecs', you can be sure that the claims are wholly misleading and false. Based on stacks of debunkable assumptions about light, atoms and gravity, and a totally mistaken conception of the realm we live in and how stuff works.

Light years, the idea of light travelling through space for an entire year (or millions of years), is patently absurd. Even if it were possible you would never be able to see it. Light is not 'photon particles traversing outer space', light is Fire, it is vibration in the Aether. It diminishes in amplitude *rapidly* with distance.

People see lights moving in the sky and falsely believe them to be 'satellites', but according to the globe model, the *minimum* height for a satellite to achieve orbit is about 180 miles. It is simply not possible to see a small device in the sky *at night* from 180+ miles away, whether it has lights on it or not, the angular resolution of the eye is exceeded.

I am, however, well aware that there are mysterious 'UFO' moving lights in the night sky, I've seen them. I don't know what they are, but I *know* they are not tin cans in free fall at 180 miles away (Sky TV satellites are said to be orbiting at 26000+ miles!).

If 'planet earth' and the 'solar system' were moving through 'outer space', the relative positions of the stars would be changing constantly. The night sky would be different every day, every week, every year, but it's not, the angles of the stars are fixed, the constellations are the same now as they've always been. The ancients knew that the stars didn't move from their angles, this is why they specifically called them **the fixed stars**.

The true nature of the stars has been occulted by Jesuit heliocentric dogma, the 'sci-fi industrial complex' and the farcical 'space programs' of NASA, ESA, Space X, and the like, which serve to brainwash and deceive the populous on an industrial scale.

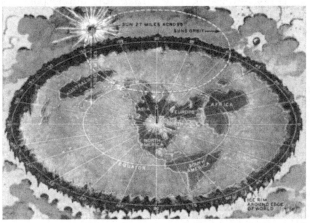

Wilbur Glenn Voliva map (1931)

Chapter 8

Why I'm Not An Astronaut

If it was even remotely possible for me to be an astronaut, I would have been one. I was that kid who could achieve anything I put my mind to, and I wanted to be an astronaut (what kid wouldn't?). It's a cruel and sinister deception however. The so-called 'space agencies' of the world have been running a massive scam since the 1950s, a ruse to convince the world that they have been exploring the universe, sending astronauts and satellites into 'orbit' and around 'the planet,' and so on.

Unfortunately there is no easy way to break this to people. It's like a Santa Claus moment for grown-ups, but it's very important for our spiritual development that we understand this deeply; **space exploration is a lie**. At one point in life, I actually believed I had a chance of becoming an astronaut, being as I was, an astrophysics guy. But no, it turns out you have to sign your soul away to the military and go through years of intensive 'psychological training' (brainwashing). Astrophysics isn't even a prerequisite (it's not even useful in space).

The most important quality an aspiring astronaut must possess, is the ability to go on television and tell big fat barefaced lies to the public, and be ok with it. You see, the whole 'space race' is a reality TV show that started with the creation of NASA in 1959 (see 'Operation Paper Clip') and the signing of the Antarctic Treaty. It continues today with SpaceX taking the current focus.

When the government can't be bothered to keep the space charade going, there's always a billionaire entrepreneur willing to come along and take the lime light (remember Virgin Galactic?). There's lots of glory to be gained from blowing stuff up in the name of space exploration, *the future of humanity depends on it*, and it helps if you have money to burn.

Rocket science is touted as another peak intellectual achievement of humanity, like nuclear physics and so-called vaccines. But when you get down to brass tacks, every rocket ever launched is basically just a highly expensive fire cracker that blows up and goes nowhere. Most of them explode in the air or crash down into the ocean. Yet, due to the spell of heliocentric indoctrination, there are millions of people who salivate over every thrust of a rocket engine as if it brings them one step closer to a new life on an alien utopia floating among the stars. They are looking at fireworks and believing in fairytales.

Rockets do make for effective guided weapons however, and it has been suggested that these rocket programs may be part of an effort to crack open the firmament and break out of the realm, like a modern day tower of Babel. Operation Fishbowl (1962) was apparently one such effort, a series of 'nuclear' missile detonations in the sky above the pacific ocean near Hawaii. The maniacs who did it were considerate enough to aim the missiles a little bit south of the islands, and to do it in the daytime to avoid afflicting the entire population with radiation blindness.

The cover story tells us they were just harmless nuclear blasts to 'probe the upper atmosphere', or a cold war response to soviet sabre-rattling, but it turns out that 'probing the upper atmosphere' is globe-code for 'shooting nukes into the firmament'. After this, they made up the notion of the Van Allen belt, which became like the atomic terminology for the firmament.

The first commonly consumed image of the globe was in the Universal Studios logo at the start of movies, but the first alleged photograph of the globe was published by NASA on April 1st 1960, and though it turned out to be the most legendary April fools prank in history, not too many people seem to remember it.

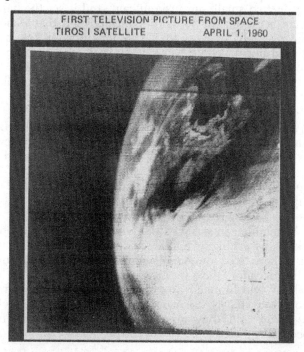

FIRST TELEVISION PICTURE FROM SPACE
TIROS I SATELLITE   APRIL 1, 1960

The award for best Best April Fool Ever goes to NASA, for the 'first television picture from space'. But the biggest prank of all, the one that really got to people, was of course the televised moon landing of 1969, something that is still taught to children today as the peak achievement of humanity, though it has been debunked endlessly and looks more ridiculous with each passing year.

Many people see it for the hoax it was, but many are still clinging to it and all it represents. The "boomer" generation (those born between 1946-64) would have been sat in front of the goggle box as children, watching the grainy footage live, living the dream, and having no reason to question its authenticity.

It is a particularly insidious spell which has had severe spiritual consequences on several generations. It took people far far out of their own hearts and minds, out of reality, a quarter of a million miles into the void. It made them feel so small and insignificant, and it set the bar of human achievement so astronomically high that nobody could possibly live up to it (nothing greater has been achieved since). People even say things like "we went to the moon", as if they themselves rode along with the astronauts in the Apollo, driving the buggies, planting flags and playing golf in the dusty grey desert.

I'm a Generation x/y crossover kid, I became skeptical of the moon landings as a young student, but I still believed that everything else done by NASA was legit; the deep space probes and the mars explorations, Voyager, the Hubble telescope, etc. I believed in all that. This turned out to be a naive and logically fallacious position.

When I began seriously studying NASA's own content with a discerning eye, the evidence of chicanery was everywhere to be found. Lots of people have been calling it out for decades. They are disparagingly referred to as 'flat earthers' and branded as crazy lunatic fringe conspiracy theorists by the NASA-worshiping media, but the fact is *they exist*, and they are *extremely meticulous* in their research.

Every image that NASA produces is both easily faked and scientifically useless. Their live broadcasts of 'astronauts' in space are extremely patronising and ridiculous. Show me the face of an astronaut and I will show you the face of a military trained liar. The whole thing is one big dirty counter-intelligence operation. These people are not exploring or discovering anything, they are *acting*, and they are *mocking you*. Anthony Kiedis said it straight up in the hit Red Hot Chilli Peppers song 'Californication', *'Space may be the final frontier but it's made in a Hollywood basement'.*

Though there is a *lot* more that can be said on the topic of 'faking space', I don't wish to dwell on it, since it is the least interesting aspect of the whole story I am presenting here. It has been covered *many* times before in video format, in greater depth than I ever could or would want to[1]. There are myriad channels and documentaries devoted to it online who do a perfectly fine job of exposing NASA lies and the globe conspiracy, and the reader is encouraged to dive deep[2].

Beware that all the controlled media platforms such as Youtube are now highly censorious of flat earth content, and will always saturate search results with pro-globe videos, and patronise you with a warning that 'flat earth is an archaic conception of the world.'

Key Implications of the Globe Hoax

Here we will summarise some of the important conclusions that have come out from all the research in recent years. It is not meant to be exhaustive but this at least covers the fundamentals:

- Every picture/video/model of the globe earth is a fabrication.

- Globes are not for educational purposes.

- The ocean horizon line is always observed to be flat/level.

- Ships that disappear 'over the horizon' are seen again with zoom lenses.

- The stated curvature (8 inch per mile squared) is not observed.

- Earth is not a planet or an object, it's the ground, it's your flesh.

---

[1] Check out *Jeranism, Witsit Getsit, Globebusters, Spacebusters, etc*
[2] *What on Earth Happened*, 13 part documentary series by *Ewar Anon*

- The north pole is the centre of the realm, not the sun.

- Gleason's map provides the best view of the territory.

- The great ocean is flat like a giant circular puddle.

- Antartica is an ice shelf surrounding the 'edge of the puddle.'

- The land is stationary and immovable within the water.

- North is 'in' and South is 'out.'

- East is anti-clockwise, west is clock-wise.

- Sun & moon move in spiral paths above the earth plane.

- Gravity is a fictitious force.

- Nobody landed on the moon. Moon is not Earth.

- There are no orbiting satellites (just balloons, drones and aircraft).

- NASA weightless videos are filmed in vomit-comet aircraft.

- Astronauts are bad actors, liars, counter-intelligence agents.

- Rockets are fireworks.

- There is no Tesla in space, and no telescopes either.

- There is no outer space, its all inner space.

- Pressurised air implies we're in a Hermetically sealed container.

- Stars are not nuclear, and they're not millions of light years away.

- Planets are not 'lands', they can't be landed on or conquered.

- Nobody is going to Mars on a rocket, Mars is not a land.

- President Nixon didn't phone the moon from a rotary dial in 1969.

- The Space Force appears to be a front for the Air Force (space = air)

All the international space programs are fraudulent too, and they exist for the same reason. The Americans have the biggest budget for it, they've capitalised on it the most through Hollywood and TV, and making NASA into an idol. But if the western space propaganda still seems believable to you, try looking at Russian, Chinese, Indian or even Israeli or North Korean footage. From the greatly reduced quality and tackiness of their productions, you will surely snap out of the spell and realise that its all about mind control and keeping people asleep.

Ultimately the promise of space exploration is a substitution for religious salvation, an escape from our predicament here on this 'finite planet'. So NASA/SpaceX and the like have been rightly described as 'church for atheists.' It provides a focal point of false hope for the faithless to pour their worship into, while satan rubs his greedy hands at all the loosh and needless destruction. It's no coincidence that rockets are a blatant phallic symbol too, this is part of the mockery of rocketry, it's penis worship by proxy.

There is really no need to be blowing stuff up with rockets, if you want to go straight up you need only use Hydrogen or Helium gas balloons. Indeed, NASA is the world's largest purchaser of Helium, and this is how so-called satellites actually work. They do not orbit an imaginary spinning globe, but rather they are floated up on balloons called *satelloons* (like the infamous 'Chinese spy balloon').

The space-exploration-by-rocket narrative seems to be a kind of ritual theatre carried out by counter-intelligence agents from the likes of the CIA and MI5/MI6, and directed by shadowy Jesuit hands (who also own all the big telescopes by the way). These agencies work closely with Hollywood, academia and media to reinforce heliocentric and atomic dogma in TV and movies.

Blockbuster movies such as Gravity, Interstellar, and Oppenheimer are manufactured specifically to propagate and give credence to the theory of gravity, to Einstein's theories of general relativity (time dilation and bendy space-time featured in Interstellar) and nuclear energy (E=mc2, the theoretical basis of 'the bomb'). Hollywood makes it more believable than the academics can.

The government are actually quite terrible at faking space. Once you can see through the spell, the 'space news' section becomes pure comedy gold. There is an endless stream of fake space news that is spun out on the MSM and social media. It masquerades as science but it is pure mockery, loaded with patronising condescension and sexual innuendos.

The videos of astroNOTs floating around in a phoney space station with big hair and random wires all over the walls, performing trite demonstrations of weightlessness, are all filmed on vomit-comet aircraft. It's a pantomime. The HD videos on Apple TV, flying over the globe from the ISS space station, with all the street lights glowing intensely on the lands below, lightning going off in the clouds and the green haze auroras on the curved horizon below a starless sky, pure CGI. People are being brainwashed with false images.

All that would be needed to prove the globe would be to film the horizon while going straight up in a balloon. It would start flat at eye level then as you ascended it would bend at the sides and curve down and away as you got higher up. Nobody has been able to reproduce this, even SpaceX with all the dozens of rocket launches they claim to do. Never produced this simple footage of the flat horizon continuously bending into a sphere, their cameras always point at the rocket. We learn nothing about the cosmos from these experiments. It's just pure rocket porn.

There are several amateur high altitude rockets that have produced continuous video footage up to 120,000ft where the horizon remains totally flat at eye level. Even one that appeared to get stuck in the firmament. Globe sticklers will claim that continuous raw amateur footage is fake, while holding strong that NASA's piece-wise TV footage is all legit. Truly I tell you, all NASA footage is *unfalsifiable* and *unverifiable*, it's not scientific in any way at all, it proves *nothing*. It's a deflection from what is really going on.

As technology progresses the globe deceivers get more 'sophisticated' with their fakery, using better graphics and AI and so on. It's still quite easy to discern the hoax when you realise there are still *no fruits*; nothing has come from the space program except lies, false hope and delusion.

It doesn't matter how realistic they make the CGI, or how big the rockets they make, or how many smutty news stories they publish about *Uranus*, none of it ever leads to anything. It never produces any benefit for mankind, it's a pure dog and pony show, fantasy, wishful thinking, a LARP for atheists.

Chapter 9
Hawking Isn't Talking

Isn't it weird that E=mc2 is the most widely recognised physics equation in the world? And yet it is literally of no use to anybody. This is the power of propaganda. Most people can't convert miles to kilometres, but they sure know all about E=mc2!

Everyone knows about Albert Einstein, he's the greatest genius who ever lived, right? Followed by Stephen Hawking, of course! You can't argue with that, they are the two most brilliant minds in the entire history of the human intellect *ever*. Their contributions are greater and more significant than all the other achievements of all lesser mortals combined!! They are truly *GODS AMONG MEN!!*

Seriously though, you have to wonder why these two odd fellows are given such pride of place in the pantheon of academic idols. I used to admire them myself, but as I've alluded to previously, I was a naive young fool, an idealist.

The fact is, when you no longer worship atoms and

gravity as your personal lord and saviour, and you're no longer awe-struck by academic laurels, waffly explanations or synthesised speech, you start to see more clearly what is right in front of your face.

In the cold light of day, it is plain to see that neither Einstein nor Hawking achieved anything meaningful by tinkering with their tensors, it was all pure vanity, indulgent mathematical conjecture, mental gymnastics and CGI razzamatazz. Relativity is *not reality,* and absolute truth exists *absolutely.* Gravity and/or 'bendy-space-time' are not found in nature, they are mathematical models with no useful application in the real world, and this is what Stephen Hawking devoted himself to.

In 1963 at the age of 21, he was diagnosed with terminal ALS and given only 24 months to live, yet somehow he managed to press on for *55 more years.* People with ALS (a.k.a Lou Gehrigs or Motor Neuron's disease) only live 3-5 years max, he outlived them all by more than *10x.* That is quite an achievement. Something was surely working for him. He looked healthier and more plump in 2016 than he did in the 1970s. He somehow developed golden blonde hair and grew a new set of teeth in his old age (despite being unable to eat solids for decades).

Now before I get accused of distasteful humour or 'ableism', it's important to understand the reason for my sarcasm. It has come to light in recent years that the Stephen Hawking 'phenomenon' is actually something quite sinister and disturbing, so I'm using bits of humour to relieve the tension, otherwise it would be too depressing.

I am not the first to say it, and I won't be the last, there have been several presentations about it online (banned from youtube of course, but search Bitchute or Odyssey), and even some coverage in the mainstream media[1]. Most recently (2024), there were some bizarre revelations regarding his appearance on Epstein Island, so there's a LOT of things about Hawking that just don't add up.

---

[1] https://www.dailymail.co.uk/femail/article-5261939/Has-Stephen-Hawking-replaced-puppet.html

The charge against him is that the man we see in the wheelchair is, in fact, not a scientific genius but merely a puppet. A stooge that gets wheeled out by the establishment to give intellectual credibility to political agendas. He is not the one programming the words on the computer. The voice is scripted by hidden hands, crafted behind the scenes then attributed to Hawking via the speaker on his wheelchair.

We are expected to believe Hawking did all his greatest work by twitching the inside of his cheek in binary code to program a speech synthesiser with the words he wishes to say. Try to imagine that! Theoretical physics is hard enough when you have the ability to *write* and *draw* and *communicate*, how much more challenging must it be while in a state of total physical and verbal paralysis, limited to using 1s and 0s? The only conclusion, he must be a *super-genius*, right!?

Though severely disadvantaged, Stephen Hawking did have one big advantage over everybody else in the world, he can say anything, and nobody can challenge him. Nobody can argue with a mute in a wheelchair, it's just not fair play. It would be cruel and 'ableist' to rebuke him, plus you'd be waiting forever on him to program responses with his cheek muscle. But, can he even really do that? I used to wonder why we never saw him in live debate or conversation with people, but it makes sense now, all the words emanating from the computer voice are pre-programmed, he can't come up with real-time responses on the fly, that would be crazy. At best he can select phrases from a preset list.

But does he even do that? How much input does he really have on the words that come out the machine? We have all witnessed him sat there with that gummy smile while the synthesised speech buzzes out science words, we may even have seen him twitching a joystick with his wrist a few times, but we've never seen him *actually communicate*.

Nevertheless, his extreme disability status gives him virtually unlimited credibility in academia and on the world stage. In the inverted realm of legacy media, it's all about the victim. The more of a victim someone is, the more exalted they are. Stephen Hawking is the undisputed champion of the victim olympics.

We are told he was the greatest physicist in the world at just age 19. He experienced a lengthy decline in bodily functionality throughout the 60s and 70s and had to give up lecturing, but his mind remained sharp and his determination to uncover the secrets of black-holes was unwavering. However, something happened in 1985 that changed his life forever.

While at a conference in Geneva hosted by CERN, he fell ill with pneumonia and was rushed to hospital, put on a ventilator and given a tracheotomy which destroyed his throat rendering him unable to vocalise even the most basic groaning sounds (which he had been using to communicate through the 70s). Allegedly, he was then shuffled off back to England to be managed by a team of professional carers.

A year later he emerged, reborn, like a phoenix from the flames, equipped with a highly advanced (for the time) custom voice computer and wheelchair. In 1988 he published his seminal work 'A Brief History of Time', the most successful and unmemorable pop-science book ever.

He then went on to be a celebrity science idol for the next 30 years, appearing in a myriad of TV shows, movies, adverts, pop songs and concerts, touring universities lecturing, even going up in a "zero-g" vomit-comet aircraft in 2007 to experience weightlessness. For someone who can't move a muscle, or talk, he's a serious 'mover and shaker', a super hero on wheels, he gets around!

He's also a bit of a ladies man. He has been accused of fondling handlers and seducing nurses with his charming banter. His condition did not hold him back sexually. He got married and supposedly produced three children in the years after his crippling disability kicked in (try not to think about that too much). Then in 1995 he got divorced and hooked up with one of his carers, someone named Elaine Mason.

Now I don't like to judge by appearances, but Elaine Mason is a very suspicious looking individual who comes with a very suspicious back story.

Elaine, as the story goes, was previously married to David Mason, the engineer who developed Hawking's voice box. Think about that for a second; she divorced a successful able-bodied engineer who can speak, and married a paralysed mute in a wheelchair who relies on her ex-husband's technology to talk! Before that, she was just a humble nurse at an orphanage in Bangladesh, helping poor children out of the kindness of her heart.

After his divorce was completed in 1995, Stephen wasted no time getting right back in the game. Elaine had been one of his nurses/handlers for quite some time, so she was well familiar with his ... proclivities.

Though this was during the peak of his celebrity career, their relationship was reportedly strained, mired by rumours of abuse and cruelty. It lasted until 2006, at which point "Elaine" dropped off the face of the earth, never to be seen again, probably back caring for the poor orphaned children in Bangladesh.

Curiously, all the tabloids put out stories around the same time with headlines like 'All you need to know about Elaine Mason', where they lay out the whole list of sanitised, government-approved factoids. The spell being cast in those articles is clear; *there is nothing more to know about her than what we tell you.*

If I were a gambling man, I'd be willing to bet my bottom dollar that Elaine Mason is an undercover agent, a military man in a ginger wig, possibly even a 'catch & release' criminal. Serial liars like this have a very distinctive face that becomes easy to spot as you get wiser, plus you have to be seriously lacking in morals or under huge amounts of blackmail pressure to pull off a stunt like that.

The more you look, the more it starts to seem like the people surrounding Hawking are impostors and agents, bad actors playing a role in some twisted secret narrative, using him like a prop or a 'cash cow', a way to advance their careers and fill their pockets.

His alleged sprogs, Timothy and Lucy Hawking, are also quite suspicious. They have done the rounds on all the UK breakfast shows, tabloids and magazines, retelling their fond childhood memories about how he was the greatest dad ever, and cashing in on all the book sales and royalties of course. It must be said, they bear no similarity to Stephen at all. He was not exactly a handsome man but he had very distinctive primate-like features which did not seem to pass on to his children (lucky for them).

There is some video of Hawking "actually talking" prior to his accident, but I warn you, it is disturbing to watch. He is just groaning incomprehensibly, with nothing even close to words coming out of his mouth. Yet his trusty "interpreter" dutifully translates it all into perfect English, *"he says that no light can escape from the gravitational pull of a black hole."* It's a very ballsy charade and I will admit, I fell for it. I was an ignorant fool for ever believing this man was a genius.

When dealing with long-term media narratives like this, where information is based solely on testimonies of actors and compromised people, or something that was once uttered by a computerised voice machine, it can be hard to know what is true or genuine. However, when all the tabloids and breakfast shows are telling you the exact same list of 'facts', we know for sure it must be bought and paid for, a total fabrication.

Perhaps the most bizarre twist in the life of this "tortured genius" was his association with the Jeffery Epstein/Mossad honey-trap operation. There are several pictures that have emerged with him on the island hanging out with some very unsavoury characters. It turns out Jeffrey Epstein was a big supporter of scientism, he branded himself as a 'science philanthropist', among other things. In 2012, he financed a conference in the US virgin islands[1], with 21 of the worlds "top physicists", including

---

[1] www.pr.com/press-release/401973

Hawking, and his able-bodied Canadian counterpart Lawrence Krauss, and three Nobel laureates, with the purpose to "define gravity" (but wasn't it defined 350 years ago?).

In January 2024, there was a large publication of files relating to the Epstein case, including transcripts of a conversation where it is claimed that one of Hawking's proclivities involved 'watching naked midgets try to solve complex equations on a blackboard too high up'. Of course this is pure gossip, information that could be easily fabricated, and actually totally ludicrous the more you think about it. There's no way to know if he really said or consented to anything at all.

Understand that it can't be determined whether Hawking was ever even sentient, whether he wrote any of the books or said any of the things attributed to him. There is no evidence that he was capable of communicating his 'proclivities' to anyone. It is absurd to even think of a man in that position as having 'proclivities' and going to a sex island to partake in orgies, it's pure mockery.

Quite possibly he has been inserted into the Epstein narrative to distract from the other living men and women who are implicated in it, or he was just brought out to the conference for 'shits and giggles'. Epstein is said to have specially modified his personal submarine for Hawking's arrival.

It's entirely possible that the figure in the wheelchair was in some cases not even a living man, but due to the extremely limited degree of bodily movement on display, it could have been animatronics. It appears there were several different 'models' of Hawking used over the years, maybe 3-4 different versions of the body in the chair. People note the changing hair colour (from black to grey to golden blonde), weird teeth developments, ear size, nose shape, skin quality, and so on.

The prevailing theory is that the 'real' Stephen Hawking died during the Geneva incident in 1985, and what emerged after that was some kind of Frankenstein's monster, a state-controlled bionic boffin, the Robocop of Physics (curiously Robocop was released right around the same time).

A Brief History of Time was likely written by a team of ghost writers. It's very waffly, and his computer speech would be programmed by whomever happens to be 'using' him at that time. This was evident in the later years as he began spouting globalist rhetoric and pushing political agendas, appearing in ever more bizarre places like Star Trek, Stargate, The Simpsons and Futurama. But his core message and philosophy was always essentially the same; there is no god, aliens are real, the planet is going to die from climate change, and gravity will suck us all into a black hole.

We may never know exactly what happened with him, or who Elaine Mason really is, or whether Timothy and Lucy are really his children (his first wife Jane was admittedly having affairs), but we can be sure of two things; he made no fruitful contributions to science, and the official story of his life is a charade, a mockery.

It is a mockery of the idolatry of scientism. The joke is that the idolaters are essentially worshiping a 'retard' whom they believe is a genius. But he clearly has no more capability than a vegetable. It's a mockery that shows how unscientific and gullible the majority of scientism believers are. As someone who was very much involved in that world, I feel it deeply. It's a cruel mockery but it perfectly illustrates the folly of idol worship.

I used to think Erwin Schrödinger was an idol, because of his *legendary* quantum wave equation and the infamous cat paradox, I even quoted him and used his image in presentations. Then I found out he was a rampant pedophile! It would have been good to know that *first*, before quoting his work and associating myself with him, but the world is an inverted place, and it seems academia is generally unconcerned with morality these days.

It's notable that the word *hawking* means *selling in a public place by calling out to people.* As in, *merchants hawking their wares,* or *media hawking their narratives,* or *scientists hawking their theories.*

If, as I suspect, this whole thing is a mockery, then the deceivers might have left a few little "easter eggs" or clues for inquisitive truth seekers such as ourselves. Well, get this. It just so happens that Stephen Hawking died on March 14th 2018, also known as 'Pi day' (3.14), a poignant date for physics geeks, which also happens to be ... *Einstein's birthday!!* And if that weren't unbelievable enough, we're told that his friends at school used to call him by the nick-name ... 'Einstein'.

Of course, we're expected to believe that this all happened by sheer coincidence on the edge of a giant spinning ball of atoms in an uncreated universe devoid of meaning and intelligent design!

To the discerning eye, it is quite evident that the story of Stephen Hawking is a fabrication, and a profitable one too. There was never any real physics being done, nobody will ever use one of Hawking's equations to solve any real problems. It's all complete gobbledegook designed to make gravity seem like this super complex thing that only the most tortured boffins can comprehend.

Actually it's not so complicated, the plain truth is very simple to understand. Gravity does not exist in nature, never has, never will, it has no place in true science and should be banished from our vocabulary altogether.

Hawking is to Einstein as Einstein is to Newton. They are the 'gatekeepers of gravity'. Nothing can be said about gravity without invoking them. They *are* gravity, and this is why they are held up above all other men of history. Without gravity, the Copernican model of the spinning globe earth and the Heliocentric solar system fall apart, along with the entire field of astrophysics and the whole state-sanctioned history of the universe. The big bang, the explanations of stars and galaxies, the planetary globe model, and even the theory of evolution. All of it collapses like a house of cards.

Chapter 10

Evolution, the Evil Illusion

The theory of evolution can seem reasonable and logical at first. I used to accept it to some degree when I was a student of scientism. Many people have accepted it as gospel now for 150 years or more, even in religious circles. However, as I transitioned from a scientific career to being an independent artist, it also brought a radical shift in perspective. I began to see everything in nature as a work of art, an act of *creation*. The theory of evolution is directly opposed to this idea. Given the premise of this book, we might even say that evolution *occults* creation.

Creation is an alchemical process. It is an artistic and scientific endeavour, deliberate, and thoughtfully conceived, measured, balanced, crafted with care. It's an act of intelligence, a labour of love, a conscious choice. Anyone who has made art purely for its own sake will understand this. It is innocent, playful, and yet skilful, determined, drawing on the full imaginative capabilities of the soul.

Evolutionary theory is designed to explain away

creation. We're told it is an extreme long-term gradual transmutation of life from the most basic atoms into molecules into the vast variety of species we see today. It is a 'bottom-up' theory of the origin of life, where species come about through the unconscious fumbling of matter, blind trial and error. Creation is a 'top-down' process, things come about through conscious intention and creative deliberation.

Creation is not some archaic idea or a fancy new science theory, it's something we actually do, something that happens. We are creative beings, I am creating as I type. It is a certainty even the most stone cold atheist can't deny. Creation and creativity exists, it occurs, it's happening.

Evolution though, is something much more ephemeral. Its not a *thing*, its more like a story or myth. The word is sometimes falsely used to mean 'gradual change', 'learning', 'adaptation' or 'growing', as in *'my writing has really evolved in the last year'* or *'I love the evolution of your music over the years'*, but these are colloquialisms, informal and incorrect use of the word. It means something much more than that, evolution is a story of our origins as a species, it goes right to the meaning and value of human life and the history of the realm. Evolution is a religion.

The theory of evolution asserts that atoms wiggled themselves into molecules, assembled themselves into cells and multi-cellular organisms, and eventually into bigger and better creatures until manifesting the whole cornucopia of life that we see today, including humans. But crucially, the atoms did this *all by themselves*, they had no spiritual or divine guidance because none of that stuff exists. All they had was Gravity (praise be), who pulled all the dust together to make the stars and planets, then Evolution (praise be) who transformed the earth and the waters into plants, animals, and humans. You see, the evolutionary theory is a creation myth with the creative process removed. We call it an 'evil illusion' not only because it sounds like it, but because that's *exactly what it is*.

The illusion of evilusion hides the alchemy of creation. It erases the creative spirit from the universe. The meaning of life is reduced to one of pure animal survival. Morality is once again chucked out the window. It's survival of the fittest, dog eat dog, you only live once, etc.

When we look at different species of life, there are common factors, features and similarities between species. Evilusion theory claims there are ancestral connections because of this. It must be understood that anatomy is universal. *Everything is basically a mouth.* The anatomy of all creatures are related to the anatomy of man because man is the *microcosm*, the universe in miniature. All lifeforms are variations of the same divine pattern. Just because we have a similar anatomy to apes does not imply that we 'evolved from' apes. In fact 'ape' means to *imitate*. They are our imitators in the animal kingdom not our *cousins.*

In the biblical story of creation, all creatures were named by Adam, the first man. In the evolutionary myth, the early universe was an empty place, devoid of consciousness, a barren landscape with nothing more than slime-moulds and 'protein chains' flopping about on the jagged space-rocks, and it was like this for billions upon billions of years. Though this is commonly accepted, it is a very extreme set of beliefs. Evolution theory was a major nail in the coffin for a lot of religion, it became the number one justification for people disbelieving in God. Prior to Darwins theory, it was quite hard to be an atheist and justify it intellectually, but now, people had their justification: *I believe in Darwin, it was all made by evolution.*

Ironically, Charles Darwin, the man credited for this, actually had an incestuous marriage with his first cousin (as did Einstein) and produced several mentally and physically defective children, three of whom died in infancy. And this is the guy who wrote 'on the origin of species by natural selection.' You'd think he would have known of the perils of incest and perhaps 'selected' a more 'natural' choice of wife, but maybe he just didn't care.

The evolutionary myth of creation can be expressed quite succinctly as "**from goo to you by way of the zoo**", which is the title of a 1984 book[1] that exposes the theory for the gigantic fraud that it is.

Schools & Fish

Evolution dominates schooling in the secular west. Though many of us think of schools and universities as a benevolent or even necessary force for the development of our children, we have to seriously reconsider this assumption in light of recent revelations. Schools have been wholly compromised with false doctrine. Most of them are centres for marxist indoctrination, peddling fake science, false history and woke ideology while driving young people into anxiety, depression and crippling debt before even starting their careers.

It is not healthy for a child's development, that they be put into a facility where they are taught that their ancestors were chimpanzees, and they must repeatedly wash themselves because they are dirty little 'disease-vectors' covered in 'germs'. This kind of treatment will cause major psychological problems later in life, and we could argue that it is deliberately designed to inhibit their development into spiritual maturity and condition them into functional NPCs.

When you dive deep into it, there is something very fishy about school. Of course the word 'school' means a group of fish all swimming in the same direction, as is the intention for the children's minds to be aligned with the state. As a former fish keeper myself I can tell you something about schools of fish; they multiply, they're always hungry, they produce a lot of shit and they're not all cute. In the wild, many of them would get picked off by predators, a natural pruning process that keeps the size of the school within certain limits, but in an artificial environment they can breed like rabbits and quickly pollute the environment. In these situations a culling

[1] From Goo to You by Way of the Zoo, by Hill, Rogers, Harrell

becomes necessary. The excess must be discarded to save what's good, such is the responsibility of one who manages whole populations.

Though I don't condone eugenics in humans it is an unpleasant fact of life that it goes on and the school system has a part to play in it. The people who built this system view us as mere cattle on a farm (or lower, *fish in a school*). The IQ test was developed specifically for eugenics purposes by one of Darwin's cousins (not his wife though, another one), to rate children with an intelligence quotient, to identify and eliminate the 'defects' and get the smart ones into secret government programs. All school exams have effectively 'evolved' from the IQ test.

There is a saying about internet apps 'when the service is free, you are the product being sold', and this is also true of public schooling. It's free because it's a sausage factory where children are minced up and shaped into compliant serfs for the state. They are cooped up and fed a pack of lies about science and history before being railroaded into a lifetime of debt, therapy, and pharmaceutical slavery.

Schools and universities in the west increasingly teach anti-family and anti-life values as part of the general population reduction effort, promoting feminism, homosexuality, climate propaganda, vaccines, and marxist ideologies. They slow the population growth by sterilisation, devaluing marriage, turning children against their parents, and pushing back the age at which couples try to conceive. Though the social sciences may be a different department from the physical sciences, they are all infused with the same ideology, which ultimately undermines the power of nations, families, and individuals for the benefit of a shadowy international death cult.

Many may cringe at the conspiratorial idea of a death cult, but it should really come as no surprise in 2024 to learn that there are powerful groups of people who conspire to make death happen at scale so that they can profit from it tremendously. This is what is meant by the 'death cult.' Genocide and eugenics are big business, maybe even the biggest business!

"Be alert and of sober mind, for your enemy the devil prowls around like a roaring lion looking for someone to devour."
~ 1Peter 5:8

Belief in evolution theory is a critical component of the cult worldview, a cornerstone of satanism. It directs government policy, which effects how public institutions treat us, how we treat children and the elderly, and distorts how we view ourselves spiritually. It is the prime justification for eugenics and ethnic cleansing, and ultimately it was used to completely change the way doctors think about sickness and disease, from a toxicological model (clean the body) to an immunological model (fight the disease).

Rebuking the modern theories of disease and medicine will be the topic of the next two chapters, then we can finally leave the sticky muck of scientism behind us and move onto part two, the marvellous and ancient art of alchemy.

Chapter 11

Germ Warfare &
Molecular Terrorists

The Theory of Evolution is the foundation for the Germ Theory of Disease, a belief system in which disease is said to be caused by particles called 'pathogens' (disease generators) which evolved out of the 'primordial goo,' specifically with the purpose to inflict undeserved suffering on human beings.

We are told they emerge from the snot of some ghastly creature like a bat or a rat, and can then hop onto other creatures, multiplying in number and mutating into new forms to evade detection. Like a shape-shifting predator from the quantum realm, a single virus is said to consists of about *5 million atoms* in a cluster, literally an atomic monster, the most massive molecule ever!

We are also told we have something called an 'immune system', which is an army of good little soldiers that defend us against these pesky molecular terrorists. Germ battles are type of internal atomic warfare, a microbiological conflict between rival molecules in the invisible realm of your blood stream.

However despite what many believe, there is actually no such *thing* as an 'immune system' in the body, and there isn't a single shred of compelling evidence for the existence of these monster molecules called viruses. Like the various flavours of particles in physics, viruses are pure conjecture, and this has been very thoroughly exposed by a great many brave doctors now[1].

Even though viruses are allegedly 'everywhere, all the time', and they are the biggest molecules ever, you cannot isolate them, you can't hold them in your hand, or capture them in a bottle or a microscope slide. Nobody can. They are and have always been, 100% theoretical, like the atoms and molecules they are allegedly comprised from.

It has become far more than just a theory though. Viruses now serve as a scapegoat for the pharmaceutical industry. Though many will hiss and seethe and contest this out of pride and attachment to their beliefs, nobody will ever come forward with proof of viruses, because there isn't any. It's not even possible.

People like to believe that everyone in the field of medicine is some saint or saviour, battling on the 'frontline' against the enemy of death and disease, but this is pure idolatry based on a flawed understanding of the causes of disease. The once sacred art of healing has morphed into a shady synthetic drug industry, a 'health care system' that is profiteering from sickness and death, steered by governments and insurance companies engaged in eugenics experiments and population control.

Good things like organic food, herbal medicine, natural healing techniques are mocked, outlawed and attacked relentlessly by the pharma-owned media industrial complex who use advertising and coercion to condition people into accepting all sorts of toxic slop, poisonous medications and mystery injections. None of which are natural or even existed before the 20th century.

---

[1] TheEndofCovid.com, massive resource over 90 doctors and researchers presenting.

Thanks to this 'miracle of modern medicine', the general health of society is at an all time low. Obesity, cancer and 'death from unknown causes' are off the charts. Excess deaths way up year on year. Athletes and celebs drop dead in middle of shows. Our elders spend their twilight years doped up on dozens of chemicals a day, a pill for every ill plus one for every side-effect of the others. Population has been forced into decline and sexual degeneracy is celebrated as a virtue. There are no elected leaders, only hollow uncharismatic career politicians and hair-brained influencers harvesting loosh from a gullible screen-addicted populous.

Sorcery & Pharmakeia

There are international groups who treat the nations as their own personal petri dish; a mass of human resource to be drugged, exploited and propagandised. These people are not alchemists, but *sorcerers*. The alchemist seeks wisdom and a peaceful heart, the ability to heal and make things better, but the sorcerer is a different kind of character altogether. Though they may share a lot of the same knowledge, and work with the same tools, they are not aligned in their morality. The alchemist is guided by nature and the word of God, but the sorcerer is a destroyer of nature and worships only himself. The sorcerer *plays God*.

The word 'sorcery' comes from the greek word 'pharmakeia', meaning 'use of spells and drugs, poisoning', and so shares a common root with with the word 'pharmacy'. Pharmaceutical medicine is real sorcery, actual witchcraft, and when people succumb to it they can become dependent on these drug-spells for *life*. You go to hospital with a sore tummy, and you come out with a lifetime dependency on some expensive, toxic, unpronounceable, petroleum-based chemical that is strictly controlled and could be fatal if overdosed. *You can't live without it.* Doctor said so.

You see it's not just a drug, there is always an accompanying *spell*. The [witch]doctor has cast a spell that *you must take the drug to stay alive.* If you take the drug and believe in it's power then you are effectively under the spell. This is sorcery. Though the culture will have you believe that sorcery is magic, like shooting lasers out of your eye balls, it's actually something far more sinister. It's about tricking people into poisoning themselves, then profiting from the chaos that ensues.

The so-called 'pandemic' of 2020 was an act of sorcery, as millions of people were led like sheep into taking a toxic mystery injection to save themselves from a phantom molecular terrorist.

Tales from the Pandemonium

It's interesting that the word 'pandemic' has nothing to do with viruses, but relates to the word 'pandemonium' which means 'abode of many demons'. This was my experience. I spent a lot of time seeking evidence of the virus, but all I found was evidence of demons and sorcery, spells and witchcraft. It was as if a portal from the nether was opened in 2020. Everything good and wholesome came under constant unrelenting attack, and it's still going on to this day. It's the 'new normal' now.

A big part of awakening is the realisation that angels and demons are a real phenomena, but aliens and viruses are not. These invisible enemies said to lurk beyond our sensory range are a trick of the demons to induce fear and turn people against each other. People become manic when they are scared of tiny invisible phantoms, like billions of little spiders crawling all over and inside of you, trying to hurt you. It's a devilish delusion.

The truth is when you are sick you don't 'have a bug.' This is a fallacy and a common colloquialism based on belief in germ theory. Viruses and all alleged 'contagious particles' are a theoretical fiction like gravity, atoms, neutron stars, or strange-quarks.

I reluctantly began researching virology in 2020. The nonsense on the news kept intensifying but the evidence was never forthcoming. I found the work of Dr Stefan Lanka. His paper "Dismantling the Virus Theory,"[1] opened

---
[1] Dismantling the Virus Theory, by Stefan Lanka

my eyes to the fundamental scientific errors and fraudulent claims inherent in virology, and led me to others such as Dr Tom Cowan[1] and Dr Andrew Kaufman[2], who have been persistently and thoroughly rebuking virology since the start. There are a great many epic resources out there such as 'What Really Makes You Ill'[3] that explain disease in terms of natural causes, without invoking atomic terrorists or genetic scapegoats.

It didn't take long to realise that there was no good reason to believe in virology, it's highly theoretical, and there was no proof of viruses to be found anywhere, not of this 'coronavirus' nor any other type of contagious disease-causing particle. Indeed, Stefan Lanka, a virologist, won a landmark court case in Germany where it was shown that there is no evidence for existence of the Measles virus, and the same is true for all viruses, they've never been proven to exist. The fundamental scientific requirements that constitute proof have not been met for any virus or contagion.

So as the pandemonium kicked off, my conscience would not permit me to comply with any rule or request that is based on this irrational fear of viruses. If I wore a mask or obeyed the rules I would be complicit in perpetuating this bogus science of virology, and validating other peoples delusions. I could not comply under any circumstances. And so began the years of persecution.

I have hardly even tried to recall what life was like during that time, it was undeniably traumatic. I feel like my mind has blocked much of it for the sake of my heart's comfort and peace. My family and I went everywhere unmasked and flagrantly disobeyed all the rules, it simply *had to be done*, given what I knew. It was real test of mettle though, a calcination of sorts. Everywhere we went feeling the heat from all angles, seeing the scornful eyes of people from behind their communist face rags.

They say 'knowledge is power', and in this instance, when you have knowledge of the fallacy of virology, it gives you the power to resist all types of germ warfare

---

[1] The Contagion Myth, by Tom Cowan
[2] Terrain Movie, True Medicine University, by Andrew Kaufman
[3] What Really Makes You Ill, by Dawn Lester & David Parker

scare-mongering. But even though I had no fear of viruses, I still had a great deal of fear to contend with. Life was like the twilight zone. Fear of a confrontation was a constant factor in stores. The biggest fear was that a scuffle might lead to all the muzzled people ganging up together and attacking me, the stuff of nightmares! So don't let me fool you into thinking I am some kind of fearless warrior. I have plenty of irrational fears of my own, it's just that 'catching a virus' isn't one of them.

For a long time the media ran vitriolic hate pieces about the unmasked and unvaccinated. The whole government-technocracy-NPC-hive-mind-complex turned on people like me, my kind. Whether it's for being skeptical of 'the science', not trusting the media or not taking the jab, for simply having faith in nature, seeking truth or even just for being a straight white man in my home country. Everything I am is wrong now. Enemy of the state.

It was a massive betrayal to process as I had worked hard throughout life to do the right thing, to learn and be positive and provide value to people and be a good guy. To help 'make the world a brighter place.' In a matter of a few weeks it all just felt like a total waste of time. Pure vanity and naivety. Like nothing I'd done mattered any more, and all my words had no effect on people.

The whole music and entertainment industry and almost every business, group and collective, even churches cucked to the tyrants and embraced the corona LARP. Many artists were selling branded face masks and using their influence to peddle the needle while thousands on social media cheered them on and congratulated them for their virtue. It was vomit-inducing and soul crushing to watch, and for a while it seemed like everyone was on board with it. Dangerous unpoked folks like me would be no longer accepted in society going forward, and I would just have to suck it up. It truly was a terrible time in history that is going to have severe repercussions for many generations.

Pandemic of Misdiagnoses

Every cloud has a silver lining though, and by late 2021 I had found a whole new community of like-minded doctors and scientists who practice natural healing and operate entirely outside of the allopathic system of medicine and the germ theory of disease. The true doctors of our time are not the pill-pushing, scalpel-wielding, ventilating, jab-happy, white-coats of the state. Rather it is those wise and brave people who have woken up, come forward, exposed the fallacies of the pharma system, and taught us in plain language how to be healthy with natural medicine and good living[1].

It turns out the belief that 'viruses cause disease' was promulgated by the Rockefeller Institute (1901) based on the claims of Louis Pasteur. It is taught to all medical students as fact, even though it has never been proven by way of the scientific method. For example, it is not possible to obtain a sample of a virus in a jar, and administer it to healthy volunteers, to see whether they all display the same symptoms. This basic test of contagion known as Koch's Postulates has never been conducted satisfactorily for any so-called virus. The PCR test does not prove or detect the presence of any viral particles. The virus is always inferred from the symptoms, because there is no way to prove its even there.

It's important to realise the implications of the testing fraud: *all viral diagnoses are misdiagnoses*, ergo **all covid diagnoses are misdiagnoses**.

People say it was 'a pandemic of testing', but you could also say it was a 'pandemic of misdiagnoses.' Literally every ailment was misdiagnosed as c-v-d for a while. You could get hit by a bus and they'd find a way to pin it on c-v-d. It was a very convenient and profitable cause of death for the National Hell Service, as well as being 'the great excuse' for people to get off work and avoid their duty of care.

---

[1] Amandha Vollmer, Kelly Brogan, Andrew Kaufman, Tom Cowan *et al.*

In the absence of physical evidence, COVID is not a *thing*. It is just an acronym representing a *list of symptoms*. When people feel unwell they experience a profile of symptoms which are then believed to be indicative of a virus.

It's all spells and wordplay. The jargon in the virus model of disease has been defined to correspond with the symptoms of detoxification (runny nose, fever, coughing etc). The symptoms we experience are real processes, we live in a highly toxic world from which our bodies regularly need to detox. But detoxification is not caused by viruses or an 'immune system'.

Furthermore, it has been shown that disease can be induced in people by the mere suggestion of it, a phenomenon known as 'psychogenic illness.' A type of 'sympathetic resonance', like how yawning can be induced by seeing another yawn (without transmission of a *yawnogenic* particle).

There is also something called the 'Nocebo effect', the opposite of the Placebo effect, where people develop a sickness due to a negative expectation. They are administered a harmless drug, then told (the spell) that it will cause sickness, and so they manifest the sickness. The power of suggestion can override the effect of drugs and produce a symptomatic response.

Given all this it seems quite clear that if the media start broadcasting a spell about some new disease, showing images of sick people, hospital corridors, lists of symptoms and death counters, then many people are going to display the symptoms of disease by negative expectation, and even sympathetic resonance with others. It would depend how responsive people are to the propaganda.

The illusion of a viral pandemic can be created through just media propaganda, snotty noses and dodgy PCR testing. No contagious particles are even necessary to pull it off.

Plausible Deniability

In the UK and other countries, there are public enquiries ongoing into the pandemonium, but not a single one of them will ever enquire as to whether there was any proof of contagion in the first place. Virology is not on trial (yet). The whole covid atrocity is predicated on the assumption that the virus was real, and they will never question that premise in order to preserve their 'plausible deniability'. The virus is the ultimate get-out-of-jail-free card for medical malpractice. It's the justification for every vaccine-induced injury and death, and countless unnecessary prescriptions and misdiagnoses. What an unholy mess it all is.

There are many reasons why people so readily accept the virus theory of disease, for doctors and nurses it provides a scapegoat. They no longer need to do any serious diagnostic or healing work, it's just a case of running the tests and following the protocols set out by the system. For the patient, it alleviates them of the burden of responsibility for their sickness. It cleverly reframes disease as a random attack by a callous invisible bogeyman, totally undeserved and unrelated to your lifestyle choices, and caused by some dirty other who you 'contracted' it from.

Note the choice of terminology there, a viral infection is something you 'contract.' But a contract is an agreement, so this suggests that you somehow agreed to it, you signed up for it? How is it you agree to be infected with a virus? You agree when you *consent* to take the test and *believe* the diagnosis. You are effectively contracting with the doctor to receive the virus. There is *no evidence* of the existence of any such thing, but you are *agreeing* to the diagnosis anyway.

Once you consent, you have signed the contract, you are under the spell. You are now obligated to believe whatever the authorities say about viruses. You must isolate, fear other people, fear children and the elderly, fear the earth and the air you breathe. Take booster jabs every month and dowse yourself in sterilising chemicals every 20 minutes. You're entirely at the mercy of the media manipulators who will run story after story about horrific new viruses and vax-induced diseases you need to worry about. Believing in viruses is a constant source of anxiety, a mental prison of torment and victimhood and it can all just melt away the moment you realise that they don't actually exist.

The End of Virology

There are significant numbers in the 'anti-vax' movement who still believe in viruses, and some have even tried to promulgate the rumour that the 'no virus movement' are controlled opposition to distract the public from the atrocities of the injections, but this is way off the mark. In fact, when you realise there are no viruses, it makes the whole vaccination agenda far more transparent. There never was a bogeyman. It was always a ruse to get the poison injections into us. In pharma land, poisoned people make for better customers, and if you happen to die then well, that's just Evolution in action. You weren't fit enough to survive, *poor you.*

Since its conception in the 1800s, the virus theory has claimed more than 200 diseases. Symptoms of disease were previously thought to be due to one of three main causes:

1. Trauma

2. Starvation

3. Toxicity

But now, due to the adoption of evolutionary germ theories, more and more diseases are defined as caused by 'viruses'. This theory has completely changed the nature of the field of medicine, from one of healing, to one of war. In the germ theory of disease, the human being is a battle ground, where molecular warfare rages on in the sub-microscopic scale; if the bad guys win then we feel bad, but if the good guys win, we feel … good. But, every time you kill the bad guys, they mutate and come back stronger, so you must keep up to date with your vaccines!

If it sounds like science fiction it's because *it is*. In the absence of scientific proof, the theory of contagious particles is a glorified superstition. It's a belief that feeds on victim consciousness, fuels societal and familial division, and creates a slavish dependency on the [Rockefeller] medical system. It also provides the *sole* justification for mass injections (cha-ching).

It has led to the infernal situation we are in now, where many medical professionals, our public servants in health, are actually afraid of sick people (and healthy people too), because they falsely believe everyone to be a potential "disease vector" or "asymptomatic carrier". This fallacy, which is now the new normal, leads inevitably to poor standards of care and tyrannical authoritarianism, as everyone is viewed with suspicion, a threat to the system. Sick people are treated like 'radioactive waste', toxic biohazards requiring sterilisation, ventilation, containment, and isolation.

It's a belief system that is not only false, but inhumane and anti-life. It creates suffering and division in society. It erects boundaries where boundaries need not be. It causes people to worry endlessly about things that do not matter, and it empowers tyrants, communists, bootlickers, and useful idiots. Nothing good ever came from virology, it's an abomination of a theory that needs to be ripped out of the tree of human knowledge like a viper, and cast into the lake of eternal fire.

Chapter 12

Shamanism &
Natural Medicine

I am not an MD, nor a "health guru", but after my PhD I spent many years immersed in the world of shamanic medicine, an ancient, universal, alchemical healing tradition that precedes the Rockefeller school by thousands of years. I have seen transformations that would be considered miraculous or impossible by hospital standards, but are commonplace by shamanic standards.

I began my journey into shamanism in the mid 2000's, attending several Ayahuasca ceremonies which were profoundly life altering. Not only did I heal some chronic physical ailments, mentally I awakened to my soul's potential, my life purpose. Spiritually I connected with the innermost aspects of self, the astral realms, after-life, and subtle dimensions.

Coming from my atheistic scientism background, this was a huge deal. It was the breakthrough experience I needed in order to confirm the reality of spirit and soul and see the folly of my materialistic ways. I was reborn in those ceremonies. I made the fateful decision to quit the 9-5, start having babies with my wife, and making music for a living. Gracias Ayahuasca.

There is a lot of information comes through during these medicine ceremonies, big downloads. It can be too much to think about or recall in the days after, but when properly integrated it stays with you, gives you a *knowing* you didn't have before, helping to inform your decisions. One of the big gifts I received from shamanic ceremonies was **faith in nature**.

I came to be completely sure that the creator exists and has provided a remedy in nature for every malady man can have. So from this point of view, whenever health problems come up, instead of calling the jab-happy white-coats at the local sorcery surgery, I look for the spiritual root cause of the symptom in an effort to eliminate it, and consult nature for a medicine to support the healing.

In cases of chronic disease, it's almost always something we are doing repeatedly that is causing it, like the 70 year old taxi driver with sciatica from sitting on his butt operating pedals all day, or the cigarette smoker who is always coughing up foul tasting phlegm. Bad habits take their toll on the body. But in cases of 'flu-like' symptoms, this is the healing process itself. It's a means of cleansing and restoring health from toxicity, so we shouldn't be fighting against it. The reason they say 'there is no cure for the common cold' is because the *common cold is the cure.* This idea that you need to fight the flu, or prevent it with jabs, is a cold-hearted scam and eugenics operation, a war against healing itself!

It can be very hard or even impossible to get people to change their habits or come round to a natural way of thinking. People often resort to painkillers, which can be fine for helping to rest, but many will take it too far, and use the painkillers in order to continue taking the actions that are causing the pain. This is not a medicinal way to use them, this is dangerous self-deception.

If, for example, we had a terrible inflammation, which

is an excess of the fire element, medicine would be something that takes the heat out of it and moistens the affected area, reducing the inflammation and allowing the tissue to heal more readily.

Healing happens when you stop taking the action that's causing the pain, and balance it out with the opposing qualities. We should view symptoms as signs or messengers that are communicating to us where we need to adjust our lifestyle.

I have also come to believe that the medicine we need most grows around us. Admittedly I can't prove this, it's an intuition, but always remember that **Earth provides**, pay attention to what pops up from the ground around you, and learn about the medicinal and magical properties of plants.

In essence, shamanic healing is a process that is achieved with four key ingredients:

1. Fasting

2. Medicine

3. Music

4. Prayer

Medicine is specifically something sourced from the plants of the Earth. In contrast to pharmaceutical 'drugs' which are patentable synthetics made from crude oil and petroleum refinement. They are like plastic medicine, designed to imitate the properties of natural medicine, but usually with lots of unwanted 'side-effects'.

Fasting prepares the mind and body for transformation. It purifies the blood and guts and lifts us up spiritually by asserting the dominance of the will over the urges of the flesh. The ingestion of the plant material kicks off an internal process which is guided by music and prayer in a sacred space or ceremonial setting. This could be a small intimate container of a few people, or a larger setting like a congregation or dance floor.

The combination of the right plants with the right music and intention can lead to profound visions, realisations and resolutions. A purging of physical and spiritual impurities. A harmonisation of the soul which ripples out to harmonise the body and life. Healing from the inside out. There are many ways to implement it, when you consider all the different possible combinations of plants, music and prayers, it is truly infinite. Needless to say this is not how medicine is practiced in the public healthcare systems of the world.

Indeed, people are often driven to the jungle in search of healing after years of being drugged out of their minds by prescriptions, cut up and passed around from one unsympathetic 'expert' to another, without success.

The reason for this dichotomy in medicine is fundamental. Alchemy tells us that men and women consist of three parts; body, spirit and soul, but modern science rejects alchemy and only acknowledges the body. Soul and spirit are deemed to be unscientific. So humans are considered as mere 'hackable animals' and treated as such.

Shamanic healing takes place at the soul level, and there is no genuine shaman or alchemist who rejects the reality of spirit. So while modern medicine may be effective at 'body work' (fixing bones and tubes), when it comes to the matters of the soul (chronic disease), it is largely ineffective, and can often make matters worse by throwing ever more drugs/surgeries/vaccines at the problem.

There is what's known as 'the paradoxical effect', a situation where the drug generates the symptoms which are used to justify more of the drug. The steady increase in drug dosage to "combat the symptoms" eventually kills the patient. The doctor/nurse may believe they are 'fighting the disease' with the drug, but actually they are fighting the healing. This is one of the ways people are being euthanised under the guise of 'care'.[1]

----

[1] A Good Death, by Jaqui Deevoy on Ickonic

The difference between healthcare and healing is; healthcare gets people *on* drugs, healing gets people *off* drugs. Healing makes us stronger, healthcare makes us more frail and dependent. This is why healing is never talked about by big pharma or media, and why some of the most common healing plants are illegal or demonised. It's bad for business.

Healing is the highest application of science. It is the expression of natural law to create effective lasting remedies to restore peace and harmony to a situation.

This principle is enshrined in alchemical philosophy as the Elixir of Life or Philosopher's Stone, which is the highest goal of alchemy and symbolises the power to heal, perfect, and make-better. Should this not be the goal of all science?

As it turns out, choosing to heal with natural medicine is one of the most spiritual and rebellious things you can do these days. Because the whole entire establishment, be it academia, media, politics, public health, corporations, and all the people who blindly follow them, are 100% sold on germ theory and viruses. They're guzzling petroleum-based drugs and shooting-up boosters like their life depends on it. They are enslaved by pharmaceutical sorcery and these are the people telling you that natural medicine is quackery.

Taking responsibility for your disease and healing with nature is a way to *lean on God* instead of leaning on man. When we look to the world of man to heal us, it usually comes at severe cost. But when we look to nature, there are great rewards for body, soul, and spirit. A true doctor is one who teaches us how to heal ourselves with nature.

In the USA you can come out of the hospital with a bill as big as your mortgage! In the UK's NHS, though the treatment is usually free, it often results in body parts getting removed, mandatory mystery jabs, increased levels of frailty and a life-time addiction to drugs. If you're lucky you might even get euthanised by one of our fabulous dancing nurses!

Natural medicine is not nearly so costly. There's never any need to inject people, remove body parts, or get them hooked on drugs. The Hippocratic principle of 'do no harm' is actually honoured.

It is a measure of the dire state of the times we live in, that something so good and pure and essential as natural medicine is so persecuted, outlawed and misunderstood by the common people.

Just as the Rothschilds control the banks, churches, and uni-party governments with the power of usury and blackmail, so the Rockefellers control crude oil, big pharma, and the medical system by the power of sorcery. There are several other ruling families of course, and I don't wish to get into all that here, but the point is just to grasp how it is that 'the few control the many'.

The big pharma corporate egregore is the antithesis of the shaman, the nemesis of the alchemist. It's anti-life, anti-healing, anti-nature, and anti-christ. A parasitic entity that has proved itself to be a mortal threat to all nations and the good people therein. It is evident that this pharmakeia has severely impacted the health and happiness of populations. It is behind the reduction in food quality and the rampant drug addiction taking over cities and towns. They control the legal and illegal drug markets, pushing billions of toxic injections into arms all over the world, and then when people start getting sick and dying, they make trillions in profit on new drugs, treatments and death-care for the vax-injured. It's a diabolically monstrous machination of misery, and we would be wise to stay well clear of it.

Natural medicine is *the way*.

"*For by thy sorceries were all nations deceived*"

~ Revelation 18:23

Part 2

The Secret Art of Alchemy

Chapter 13
Soul Science

The word 'Alchemy' is generally dissected as 'Al-chemia' (Greek) or Al-kīmiyā (Arabic) where 'chemia' (χημεία) and 'kīmiyā'(ﻜﻴﻤﻴﺎﺀ) means 'to pour' or 'to fuse/cast' as in relation to the smelting and alloying of metals. It is the origin of the term 'chemistry'. The prefix 'Al-' is the definite article in Arabic, equivalent of "The", the root of 'All', and one of the names of God as in 'Allah, Almighty, The All'.

So the fusion Al-chem suggests a kind of sacred science, not just your regular run-of-the-mill chemistry, but THE Chemistry, Holy Chemistry. It is sometimes called The Art, The Royal Art, The Great Work or simply The Work. It is said to have had its origins in Egypt, and so the 'chem' may relate to 'Khemet', an ancient name for Egypt which translates as 'the black land'. This is said to be due to the fertile black soil of the Nile valley, where most of the Egyptian civilisation was concentrated.

Khem means black, and it's no accident this should be in the centre of the word, it is of important symbolic significance in alchemy, representing the first of four stages of the great Arcananum experiment:

1.   Nigredo (the blackening).

2.   Albedo (the whitening).

3.   Citrinatas (the yellowing).

4.   Rubedo (the reddening).

The aim of the experiment is the production of a mythical substance known as **The Philosopher's Stone**. Often depicted as a ruby red crystal or smooth crimson rock, the stone is a subject of great mystery, speculation and deliberation. There are several historical accounts of its use[1], and the methods for producing it have been written about at length[2]. It is said to be notoriously difficult to achieve, something only becoming of a true master. The stone is said to have extraordinary powers and applications including:

-      Transmutation of base metals into gold.

-      Universal panacea, cure for all ills.

-      Elixir of life, longevity potion.

-      Inner transformation, spiritual enlightenment.

Many will try to tell you that the stone doesn't exist, that it's just a fantasy of mad medieval puffers trying to make gold in their mother's basement. They try to hide it's existence altogether. In the 1990s it was brought to the popular consciousness through the fictional epic 'Harry Potter and the Philosopher's Stone.' When it came time for the book to be released in the US, the name was edited to 'Harry Potter and the Sorcerer's Stone'. Allegedly this was

[1] Hermetic Museum Restored and Enlarged, Vol I-II, by Arthur Edward Waite
[2] The Book Concerning the Tincture of the Philosophers, by Paracelsus

due to marketing strategy. The publishing house Scholastic, decided that 'Philosopher' sounded too boring and academic for the savvy American audience, and would negatively impact the release, so they changed it to 'Sorcerer' to be more appealing. "It'll help sales" they said.

This one little change in the title of an epic book/movie is an act of occultism. The censors have intervened in the publication of an alchemical keyword, and replaced philosophy (love of wisdom) with sorcery (use of spells and drugs).

To be fair, the book does feature the use of spells and drugs, but the philosopher's stone is named so for a reason. It wasn't made up for fantasy and folly, it is something that has been written about at great length by alchemists for hundreds, even thousands of years. If a curious muggle were to start researching it, they might actually discover some profound knowledge. On the contrary, there is no such thing in history as a sorcerer's stone, it was literally made up to hide alchemy. Any attempt to research it will be fruitless.

Purification by Fire (and Drugs)

All the powers of the stone and all the processes in alchemy are different types of purification. During the nigredo, the raw material, or prima materia, is subjected to fiery processes such as heating, roasting, irradiating, pulverising and shaking. Intense vibrations that cause the substance to become powdered, dry, and blackened. The forcefulness of the fire element burns off impurities and reduces the material to a black ash.

Psychologically, this process symbolises the destruction of the ego through trials and tribulations. In personal alchemy, the soul is the 'prima materia' and the ego is the cloud of impure or inauthentic thoughts attached to it. Ego can be burned away by challenging circumstances and ordeals (the fire).

In this 16th century image from Matheus Greuter, the title reads '*The Medicine to Cure Fantasy, and Purging Folly with Drugs*'.

In the foreground we see an initiate having his head inserted into an oven or hearth, a fiery calcination chamber of some kind. From the chimney all sorts of images are floating out in the smoke. Armour, clothing, possessions, dreams, fantasies and foolish things. False beliefs and impure thoughts, releasing and returning to the air.

Of course, he's not literally having his head melted in some kind of gruesome ritual, you can see him waving his right hand to let us know it's all good in there. He's having his mind blown! Notably the initiate here is entering into a personal nigredo by his own free will, with the help of his comrade donning the Phrygian/Liberty Cap. He has recognised the need to purify his mind and sought help from the alchemist to do it.

Rather than clinging to the ego and fearing change, he boldly enters the fire in good faith that it was the right and necessary thing to do. This is the 'medicine to cure fantasy'.

This kind of process can be carried out with shamanic ceremonies, purgative psychedelics, as well as heat-intensive sensory deprivation practices like Temazcal, Sauna, or Sweat Lodge, that flush physical toxins out through the skin. More generally, purification can be carried out with many forms of vibratory therapies, like sound healing, music, and dance, that effectively shake the body and mind in harmonic movements to recalibrate the bioelectric field.

In the background, another alchemist is pouring liquid through a funnel into the mouth of his subject, on the bottle it reads *Sagesse*, which is old French for *wisdom*, as in 'sage-essence' or 'essence of sage'. The initiate is sat on a make-shift toilet, defecating little fools into a bedpan below. This is a depiction of 'purging folly with drugs' indicated in the title. Wisdom is poured in the head, and folly falls out the bottom.

The shelves in the background are stocked with various drugs in different types of containers. These are not the petroleum-based plastic drugs you'd find in a pharmacy, but rather, purified plant materials from mother nature, and alchemical preparations thereof, the natural medicines of an Apothecary.

The names on the labels have nothing to do with molecular structure or scientific classifications. The alchemist is not concerned with the phantasies of atomic theory. They are labelled according to **virtues of the human soul**.

Drugs serve to alter the state or condition of the soul in a specific way, and so each substance is named after the corresponding attribute it bestows upon the partaker. This is a contrast to the drugs of pharmakeia, which usually come with ugly artificial scientific names that tell you nothing about the intended effects or where it came from.

The names on the bottles on the shelves are listed below:

Top shelf:	Middle Shelf:	Bottom Shelf:
• Doctrine	• Intelligence	• Patience
• Piety	• Curiosity	• Judgement
• Diligence	• Industry	• Confidence
• Sense	• Modesty	• Memory
• Virtue	• Honesty	• Consideration
• Reason	• Good Intention	• Others ...
• Good Spirit	• Humility	
• Subtlety	• Obedience	
• Finesse	• Council	
	• Excellence	

The writings on the bottom frame of the picture indicate that through this process, even the most incontinent of men can be transformed into a sage. Incontinence here means one unable to control their lower impulses and desires, as a man unable to control his bowels.

The medicine to cure fantasy is a wild idea, but it is exactly what is needed to help people detach from the scientific brainwashing. Scientism *is* fantasy. Shamanic medicine helps banish false beliefs from our mind by lifting the veil, giving us direct contact with spirit, affirming the true nature of life and consciousness. It's not instant-enlightenment though. It's a process that takes many years of personal development, diving within and researching the ancient wisdom.

This drawing provides a visual aid and detailed instruction for transforming young fools into wise men with the use of virtuous drugs and a purifying fire, an insight into 16th century European shamanism.

Drugs & Medicine

The word 'drug' is loaded with connotations these days. It is often conflated with 'medicine' though the two are different and distinct. 'Drug' comes from 'dried' and therefore refers specifically to dried substances like salts, herbs and spices, coffee, tea, sugar, minerals, extracts, chemical pills and powders and so on.

Similarly, the word 'medicine' does not specifically refer to pills, powders or chemicals. Medicine can be anything that has a medicinal or healing effect. People can be medicine (a shaman I knew always used to say 'people are the *best* medicine'). Animals and plants can be medicine. Music, poetry, art can all be medicinal, though they are not necessarily 'dried substances'.

A drug may be medicine, but it also may not. It may be poisonous or toxic. It is more appropriate to think of drugs as **purified salts**.

Prior to big pharma and the fractional distillation of crude oil that produces the world's pharmaceuticals, drugs came from the plants of the Earth. So each of these virtues of the human soul we see on the shelves of the Apothecary are to be found as physical substances in the plant kingdom. By collecting the plants at the right time of year, drying, purifying, and transmuting the various components, we can harvest their corresponding soul qualities for medicinal use and spiritual transformation.

We may deduce, therefore, that the 'Sagesse' or 'sage-essence' that the alchemist is pouring into the funnel may not just be symbolic of wisdom, but may even be the essential oil of Sage (Salvia Officianalis), or some concoction thereof (other plants have attributes of wisdom also, like Elder, Ginkgo and Ashwaganda). Sage is used ceremonially for cleansing and purification (known as 'smudging'), and is associated with wisdom and wizardry, protection from evil spirits, enhancing spiritual connection, longevity, good health and more. Sage has all of the attributes one would need to transition from a life of tomfoolery into that of a wise man, the smell of burning sage instantly elevates consciousness, and of course the word 'sage' is synonymous with 'wise man'.

It might seem far fetched that wisdom could be bestowed upon a man by simply swallowing some plant-sauce, but in fact many people are self-initiated into wisdom and magical dimensions through the use of psychedelics like Ayahuasca, LSD, DMT, Psilocybe Mushrooms, and Salvia Divinorum (Diviner's Sage), where an irreversible change of perspective occurs following profound visions and an out-of-body experience. Even the most stubborn atheist-materialists change their views on God after a strong psychedelic trip. It has even been suggested that the word DRUGS is secretly an anagram for 'Death and Rebirth Under God's Supervision'.

Experiences like this are more potent when the body is cleansed and purified and charged with energy, so fasting and abstaining from sex in the days before is best practice. The more clean and pure a vessel you can bring to the experience, the more 'high' you can soar. Those with the most unclean vessels will have the most purging to do before they can really 'break through', and may have more confusing and challenging experiences.

Like with many things, the mainstream perspective on drugs is a distortion of the truth. Big Pharma influences almost every major institution and is the top sponsor of news and mainstream media. There are literally hundreds of thousands of toxic synthetic drugs that they are happy to give you in abundance, but there are a handful of natural ones that you're not allowed to touch or you could go to jail. It's totally inverted.

People are told that psychedelics will make them go mad, lose a grip on reality, fry their brain. But the truth is far more nuanced. Used appropriately, they can show us reality more deeply than we've ever seen it before, expanding consciousness, cleansing our minds, and helping us gain spiritual insight and wisdom.

Psychedelics reveal the dark aspects of the mind, forcing us to confront our shadow, face fears, and 'do the work'. Yes it can be maddening in the moment, when the medicine is peaking and you are hallucinating. It's scary. You can feel like reality is melting away, but it always wears off eventually. You come back to baseline, as if from a dream, changed by the experience. Facing the inner demons this way we can begin to eliminate folly and fantastical thinking, shatter illusions, break spells, and allow the mind to naturally individuate away from the 'mass formation psychosis' of the collective.

Psychedelics give us temporary shamanic powers of sight, broadening the spectrum of perceptible energy, and increasing sensitivity to light, internal and external, such that natural beauty becomes breathtakingly awesome, and evil influences are much more menacing. Normies will wake up every morning and happily watch the TV news without thinking. But if you were to take a psychedelic, stay up all night listening to great music, go for walks in the woods and dance under the moon and stars, then come home at dawn and put the on TV news, you will have a totally different perception of it, the lies and sinister manipulation will be much more transparent. Then you may reconsider your habit of watching the news every morning. Immediately the spirit is more free, less susceptible to evil influence.

This is precisely why society doesn't want you to do that. The legacy media won't tell you any positive stories of drug use because to glorify plants or psychedelics would be to threaten their profits and undermine their advertisers/ owners. Self medicating with psychedelics is a form of personal alchemy, an experiment in which we, the alchemist, are administering a drug to a subject, which is also us, and observing the sequence of events that unfolds within the body temple. Though some religious zealots will cry that this is sorcery, it is not sorcery because it is done to the self with the consent of the Self. Sorcery is malicious and used by groups of wicked individuals to deceive unsuspecting innocents, but personal healing with psychedelics is a fundamental right of any man or woman. It's a private experiment in Soul Science conducted within the laboratory of our own god-given body.

We enter into a trip in good spirit, humble, anxious with anticipation, holding intention for spiritual connection, wisdom, and self-knowledge, but open to receive whatever needs to be seen. The initial state of the mind and the intention for the trip are as crucial as the drug, the choice of music and the quality of environment. Remember, every drug is also a spell. It comes with a name and a set of words about what it is, how it works, and what you can expect from it - and the Placebo and Nocebo effects prove that words and expectations can dramatically alter the effect.

Since we are both the subject and the object of the experiment, both the alchemist (the soul) and the laboratory (the body), it comes with a fair bit of personal responsibility and it's certainly not for everyone. People new to these substances should ideally always be with an experienced friend or trained shaman.

Some psychedelics cause purging. Though it can be extremely unpleasant it really gets the deep gunk out of your system both physically and emotionally, and leaves you feeling brand new. We actually need to be sick and cry in order to heal, to eliminate toxins, and process emotional trauma.

In shamanic practice we enter wilfully into purifying ordeals with the aid of fasting, plant medicines and traditional ceremonial practices. The body is like a sponge. A vast network of pipes, tubes, capillaries and crevices, it absorbs a lot of impurities, and needs to be squeezed out occasionally or it gets clogged and weighed down. The mind also absorbs a lot information and needs to be flushed every so often, to let go of the dross.

If we don't intentionally put ourselves through purifying rituals to 'squeeze the sponge', then nature will conspire to force them upon us in the form of a detoxifying sickness ordeal, and it will be much more unpleasant and longer lasting than it needed to be if we'd done the work and gotten ahead of it.

Stages of Work

A personal nigredo can be a time of sickness, injury, chaos and confusion. A 'dark night of the soul' where external circumstances compel us to let go of old programs and beliefs. Where stubborn obstacles and limitations are imposed upon us, we 'feel the heat' in the form of fever, pressure, pain, scorn or criticism.

The initiate is humbled to the core by this fiery ordeal, and any currents of pride within him are incinerated. The nigredo leaves him charred, like purified carbon, receptive, grateful to be alive and ready to absorb higher knowledge.

The albedo, or whitening stage, represents the inflow of light into the blackened material, as it is the reception of all frequencies of light together in balance. The whitening corresponds with the moon and the lunar feminine principle, an alluring white light in the blackness of the sky, the lady of the night.

The yellowing stage, Citrinatas, corresponds with the sun, the solar masculine principle, Sol Invictus, the saviour of the day. It has been described as 'transmuting silver into gold' or 'yellowing the lunar light'. Yellow is the colour of sulphur and gold. It represents the energy in matter, the masculine soul-fire, the power of the lion.

Rubedo, the reddening, is the fourth and final stage of the magnum opus and considered a sign of having attained the perfect balance of solar and lunar energies within the substance.

So these are the four symbolic colours of the work, and their corresponding physical materials; carbon (black), silver (white), gold (yellow), the philosopher's stone (red).

Philosopher Stoned

Perhaps one of the most curious aspects of The Stone, is that its not called 'the Alchemist's stone.' Nor is it 'the fool's stone', or the magician's or the doctor's or the politician's, or the priest's or the king's or the billionaire's or even the angel's stone! It's the philosopher's stone. Why?

Bearing in mind our earlier discussion on the etymology of the word *philosophia*, we can assume there is a very specific reason why the stone belongs to Philosophers and no other group. Perhaps the power of the stone can be only be attained with a *genuine love of wisdom.* Anybody can call themselves an alchemist, just like anyone can call themselves a christian, but *god sees what's in our hearts,* and if we don't have the heart of a philosopher then the chances of obtaining the stone are slim to none.

Digging deeper into the greek word, we note that the character φ (phi) appears twice, as the leading sound in 'phi-lo' and the middle syllable in 'So-phi-a'. φ is the Greek letter corresponding to f, and in mathematics it denotes a very special number that goes by many names such as The Golden Ratio or The Divine Proportion;

$$\varphi = 1.618...$$

This number is a universal symbol of natural beauty, divine order, and perfection. It is inherent in many of nature's grandest designs, and a great deal has been said about it already[1]. It is a common factor in both love (φιλό) and wisdom (Σοφία).

This tells us that love of wisdom is cultivated through appreciation of natural beauty and good works. Philosophy is like a romantic relationship between mortal man and the eternal truth, always seeking to know more, but never able to know it all.

In the 'Creation of Adam', Michelangelo's famous fresco painting on the ceiling of the Sistine chapel, the woman under God's left arm is Sophia.

---

[1] A Beginners Guide to Constructing the Universe, by Michael Schneider

Though she may not be an "official goddess" in terms of the recognised Greek and Roman pantheons, she is the metaphorical 'bride of God', the heavenly counterpart to Mother Earth, her name suggests that the Father himself is a philosopher, a *lover of wisdom*.

Note how God is reaching out with all his might, yet Adam is laid back in a relaxed position, half-heartedly lifting his arm. This shows how God is always ready and willing to help us, it is only our lack of participation that holds us back from making the connection.

God, Sophia and the cherubs are wrapped in a shroud that is shaped like the human brain. Since the brain is the 'upper chambers' of the temple, the higher mind where God and wisdom reside.

Wisdom is a divine attribute. The scriptures tell us it is the most noble and worthy desire a man can have. When God appears to King Solomon in a vision and asks him "what shall I give thee?", Solomon replies with "an understanding heart to judge thy people, that I may discern between good and bad." (1 Kings 3:5)

From this we get the common definition of wisdom which is 'understanding and discernment' or 'the ability to judge correctly'.

As the story goes, God was so pleased with Solomon's request that he went over and above his wishes by granting him a wise heart as well as honour, riches, and length of days greater than any other king before or since.

It is considered a measure of great character and worthiness to pursue wisdom above all, for with sound powers of judgement one is better prepared to handle the responsibilities of great riches, should they be granted unto us.

For an artist, there is no more important power than the ability to discern what is good from what is not. It is the most crucial skill of all. A true artist is *someone who knows what's good*. Discernment begets judgement, judgement begets good taste, and good taste is what makes the artist.

The power of discernment relates directly to the Golden Ratio as it is the ability to accurately perceive energy, separating that which is 'golden' or 'in divine proportion' from that which is chaotic, imperfect, inauthentic, or dross.

In a spiritual sense, discernment is the ability to distinguish that which is of God (good/everlasting), from that which is of man (imperfect, temporary), and that which is of the Devil (evil/inverted).

Note that Solomon was awarded riches (gold + glory) and long life (health + regeneration), and these are the very same powers that the philosopher's stone is alleged to imbue.

Though the excessive wealth consumed him in the end, he lost his faith, and fell into moral decline later in life, Solomon is the archetype of the Philosopher-King, known for supreme wisdom and grand building projects throughout his days of glory.

Solomon sounds like 'soul of man', and perhaps this story is about our innermost soul nature. On some level we all want to rule the world, to be the Father's favourite. To get all the glory, know everything and have all the riches and live forever etc.

But is any human being really capable of handling such

power? Arguably the story of Solomon answers that question. Even the wisest king of all time couldn't sustain it, but it was his true love of wisdom that granted him the opportunity in the first place.

Chapter 14

Chemistry of Creation

It's not only physics and biology that have been 'infected' with atomic ideology, it's chemistry too. Though there are many useful applications of chemistry, it's a solid practical science, the whole field is cluttered with atomic-molecular-theoretical jargon that makes it sound way more complicated than it needs to be, and dissociates the subject from its alchemical roots.

A chemist will mix some liquids together and tell you sincerely that they 'made a molecule'. On the one hand, they did do good work by isolating and mixing the ingredients, measuring, and processing them properly, but on the other hand, they believe in this hypothetical world of atoms and molecules and 'bonds' and talk about them as if they are a fact of reality, or as if we need to know about it.

Chemists work with four things, solids (earth), liquids (water), gases (air), and heat/light (fire). They do not work directly with molecules in any 'hands on' sense. Chemical formulae are believed to represent the real physical structure of atomic molecules, but it's better to understand the molecule as a 3D abstraction representing the properties of the substance in pictorial form.

If you search the internet for a picture of DNA, you will be met with thousands of illustrations of a double helix molecule, but you won't find a single real photograph of it, why? Because DNA is a colourless liquid, it's an **acid**, known as 'aqua fortis' or 'strong water.' The double helix molecule is a fantasy of atomic theory, a hypothetical 'molecule of the soul'.

No alchemist ever worked with atoms and molecules, because there is no such thing in creation. Atoms are only of concern to people who sit around theorising, they are of no concern to people who do practical work. Despite what some scientists may claim, nobody is actually working with atoms and molecules. Atomism is a linguistic overlay, a mnemonic device. The real work happens in the transmutation of alchemical elements, earth, air, fire and water.

Chemistry is Alchemy but with the spiritual component removed. The 'Al-' has been dropped from 'Al-chem', so it's just *chem.* As we've learned already, rejection of 'the Al' is rejection of 'The All'. It leads us to worship idols, to fill the void left by the divine.

The Atom is the primary idol of scientism, a replacement for Adam, God, and the Aether, and it is the foundation upon which all vainglorious scientific theories such as gravity, heliocentrism, evolution, and virology are based. Atomism reduces the Aether to space, and Alchemy to mere chemistry. In Atomism every thing is *separate*, but in the Aether every thing is *connected*, they are diametrically opposed worldviews.

It is vitally important for our spiritual and mental health to remember that the *Aether is real.* It is so important that the architects of our language fused those two words together into **Ethereal,** which means 'extremely light or delicate, heavenly, spiritual'.

Masters of Fire

The corporate media is replete with articles that aim to smear and discredit The Art, writing it off as a quaint misguided pseudoscience from a bygone age. People I've spoken to around the world were all fed the exact same cock-and-bull story at high school, and it goes a little something like this: "*Alchemists were mad scientists long ago who tried to turn Lead into Gold to get rich quickly. They failed, but they invented chemistry in the process. The end.*"

Needless to say, there's a fair bit more to the story of Alchemy that we weren't told, like how it's a universal science of creation found in all great world cultures, and forms the hidden scientific core at the heart of religious and mystical doctrines. But let's not get ahead of ourselves.

The reason it is not taught in schools and universities is because it is occulted. This does not mean evil and wrong, it means hidden or concealed, but it's only hidden behind a very thin veil that is easily penetrated. Any sincere student with a curious and humble mind will be able to find the knowledge. It's not like it's locked in high security vaults deep underground where no one can access. It's 'hidden in plain sight,' as it were. Widely available in books and online but purposely omitted from the establishment canon of acceptable topics for public programming. In other words, you are free to read all about it, but don't expect "them" to teach you.

One who starts on the path of learning Alchemy is called an **Initiate**. Since this word is both a verb and an adjective, meaning 'to begin or set in motion', as well as 'a person newly inducted in an organisation or group', it contains a clue for the aspiring Alchemist; we must initiate ourselves.

Since we live in the real world, it is highly unlikely anyone is going to invite us into a secret Hogwartian mystery school to be trained by Masters and Adepts, so we must be self-directed, motivated from within, and if we are committed and persevering in our work then, as Carl Jung[1] said "unknown friends will come and find you".

The Alchemist is someone multi-skilled and strongly motivated, a Renaissance Man or Polymath, someone embodying qualities of the Artist-Craftsman, the Philosopher-Scientist and the Mystic-Shaman. Both spiritual and practical, the Alchemist also embodies the Smith and the Potter, those **Masters of Fire** who transform earthen ores into tools, weapons, and infrastructure for the development of society.

Smiths, Potters, Artists, Alchemists, Shamans and Mystics are the unsung heroes of culture. They fabricate durable objects, invent new materials, tools and medicines. They create songs and prayers and glorious works of art. In a thriving culture there would be many individuals occupying these roles, all working together under divine guidance. As detailed in The Forge & The Crucible[2], it is the case in some smaller cultures that all these roles are occupied by one man and his wife, holding it down for the entire community.

These practitioners of divine arts are usually always a founding member of towns and cities, for without them any attempt to build a solid settlement would be doomed to failure. They are pillars of civilisation, literally forging unbreakable materials for infrastructure and agriculture, transport and weapons, and much more, though their manner of work was often unknown, magical, and mysterious to the simple townsfolk.

This is similar to our relationship with 'big tech' today, who provide much of the pillars our modern society functions on, but their inner workings are a complete mystery to the majority of users. Big tech itself is a product of precision metallurgical work and harnessing the power of electricity and light (fire). Today's masters of fire are the masters of technology.

[1] Psychology & Alchemy, by Carl Jung
[2] The Forge & The Crucible, by Mircea Eliade

'Der Alchemist', by Joseph Leopold Ratinckx (1860–1937)

Interior of an Alchemical Laboratory, by Wellcome Images (author unknown)

The Alchemist Discovering Phosphorus, by Joseph Wright of Derby (1734-1797)

Creation is Transmutation

Alchemy is both Art and Science, but Art first and foremost. Any Artist who is fully engaged with creative work, spiritually and scientifically, drawing on their complete intellectual and imaginative faculties, will undergo thorough and irreversible psychological transformation in the process.

When the Artist transmutes the 'inner Lead' of their mental-emotional condition to an 'inner Gold' of satisfaction, glory, and illumination, Art becomes a form of Alchemy. We needn't even be engaged in laboratory chemistry experiments in order to do Alchemy, since the processes involved in the Great Arcanum are symbolic and can be applied to any type of work. In a general sense, all creative work is chemistry.

The word 'chemistry' also refers to the dynamic and ineffable sexual attraction that forms between two compatible mates. Chemistry is the precursor to love making and the creation of babies, and actually, to the creation of *anything*. But while chemistry can make many interesting things, it is alchemy that makes the **Gold**.

The word 'transmutation' means *to change thoroughly and completely*. The prefix 'trans-' means 'beyond, through, over, above', while 'mutation' means to 'undergo change in state or condition.' This is a type of change that is beyond mere transformation.

In alchemy, the pinnacle of transmutational work is symbolised by the Philosopher's Stone and the turning of Lead into Gold. We can think of Lead as representing any common, impure, or raw material, and Gold as representing the object to be attained, the desired outcome of the work, the fruits of the labour, something that doesn't tarnish, and has lasting value.

In my creative practice, I work with Digital Audio, this is my Lead. Audio is a form of data, which is an abundant resource, a 'raw material' to be harnessed and transformed. The finished piece of music is the gold, the coagulated spirit of the work. It goes out to the world via the various networks and platforms, and generates wealth in the form of passive income and business opportunities. The case can be argued that alchemists of today transmute the 'Lead of data' into the 'Gold of passive income'.

Transmutation of metal is a taboo subject in modern science. Officially it is declared to be impossible, or more specifically, according to conventional physics dogma it's *'possible with particle accelerators but requiring so much energy and cost as to make it not worth doing'* (a big fat lie to hide the truth).

But prior to the 19th century when natural philosophy was split up into physics, chemistry, and biology, it was a generally accepted principle that metals could be transmuted by purifying and blending them with the careful application of fire.

Metallurgy is not some waffly academic field of thought, it stems from generations of men who have been stood in front of raging fires all day long since the dawn of civilisation, cooking up metals for all sorts of applications. Alchemists understand metals to be created by a blending of three primary ingredients: Salt, Sulphur and Mercury.

These are not just the literal substances familiar to us, they are symbolic via their essential properties. For example, Salt does not mean 'table salt' or 'sodium chloride', it could be any powdered or granulated mineral such as Carbon or Iron, for example.

Mercury as a principle can refer to the liquid metal, or to waters and solvents in general, while Sulphur is all about the energy in matter. According to Alchemy, the combination of these three principle ingredients in varying proportions, subjected to a purifying heat of specific temperature and time, is what gives rise to the various metallic substances.

There are seven primary or 'root metals' in Alchemy. Lead, Tin, Iron, Copper, Mercury, Silver and Gold. They can be blended with each other in different proportions to create an endless variety of metallic materials (so-called 'transition metals' etc).

Iron is the only metal that does not dissolve in Mercury, which implies something very fundamental: *all metals derive from Mercury except for Iron.*

There is a wonderful quote that I heard in a presentation by the alchemist Dennis W. Hauck[1], which captures this essential alchemical truth:

   'All things dissolve into that from which they came.'

   ~ The Mahabharata

Got Any Old Gold?

Gold is considered the king of metals, the physical materialisation of the Sun. The highest, most pure and valuable of all metals, containing within it the characteristic yellow colour of Sulphur, the lustre and conductivity of Mercury, and the structure and fixity of Salt.

Gold is symbolic of Christ, the risen one. As Christ overcomes death, so the Sun overcomes the winter and the night. Gold is also associated with immortality, due to its unparalleled lustre and incorruptibility. It is claimed that eating and drinking with gold utensils confers long life and radiant health.

This may explain why the elite's of the world adorn themselves in it and hoard as much of it as they can. In the UK during the 90s-00s there were long running TV ad campaigns to get people to sell their gold. All these buyers started popping up with a cockney accent saying things like "*Got any old gold lying around doing nuffin? Come and get some **real money** instead. Treat yourself and your family to something noice.*" It all makes sense now.

---

[1] Alchemy of Consciousness, youtube channel by D.W. Hauck

It also suggests that the golden crowns and lavish jewellery worn by royalty may be a kind of protective or life extending technology (long live the king) rather than just a status symbol or display of wealth. After all, Kings and Queens come and go, but the crown persists.

History has shown that the rulers, be they mighty aristocrats or petty bureaucrats, would rather people didn't know the secrets of Gold, Silver, and Mercury. Gold and Mercury are two of the most occulted metals. School children are taught that Mercury will make them go insane, like the "mad hatters", yet for some reason dentists have no problem implanting it into our skulls in the form of amalgam fillings, and doctors are happy to inject it straight into our veins in the form of Thimerosal, a 'preservative' used in vaccines.

Many from the older generation recall playing with Mercury as children without any ill effects, but today's generation are conditioned to believe it is a toxic chemical and you shouldn't go near it. Alchemy books rarely go two minutes without mentioning Mercury, either directly or by one of it's many corresponding pseudonyms. Mercury is far more than a curious liquid metal, it is a key to great wisdom and understanding.

Chapter 15

Mercury the Messenger

Mercury is one of the most frequently talked about and mysterious concepts in alchemical lore, it has (at least) 4 different meanings:

1. The liquid metal also known as Quicksilver.

2. The divine messenger of the Roman pantheon (a.k.a Hermes).

3. The alchemical principle (alongside Salt and Sulphur).

4. The astrological planet closest to the Sun.

Though the liquid metal has been quietly occulted from the public, there is evidence of old world electrical technologies, dubbed "antiquitech", that relied on rings or bowls of Quicksilver to derive clean energy from Air or Water. Though it is presently beyond the scope of this book, if the reader were to do a deeper investigation into the electromagnetic properties of metallic Mercury, they may discover it to be a key to achieving zero-combustion free-energy, among other things.

It seems as though the Roman pantheon was culturally appropriated from Greece and other sources, and that Mercury, the Roman god of travellers and merchants, is derived from Hermes, son of Zeus, one of the Greek gods of Olympus.

Pagan pantheons were based on the visible planets in the night sky, so different pagan cultures had different names for the same light sources. Mercury to the Romans is Hermes to the Greeks, Mars to the Romans is Ares to the Greeks, Venus is Aphrodite, and so on.

Hermes also corresponds with the Egyptian deity Thoth, sometimes known as 'the first Hermes', and they are both credited with providing humanity with the sacred sciences of writing, mathematics, medicine, alchemy, astrology, and more.

It is often suggested that the Egyptian Thoth may simply be 'Thought', the universal principle of Thought itself, the mind-spring of God. *Thoth taught thought.*

If you really stop and think about it, Thought is a very mysterious thing, this internal source of light from which our words and writings flow, a virtual heads-up display in our mind's eye with which we can reason, imagine, contemplate, calculate, and communicate. Thought is a gift, a message from within.

Mercury is the messenger, a medium for receiving and transmitting divine thought. He is said to express himself in different times and eras under different names, in the same way that Thought itself is expressed through human individuals, in speech, writing, and art.

Thoth is the prime deific source of these communicative faculties, the ruler of the intellect. It is said that he is the fountain of language and the 'writer of all books'. Indeed, this very book is a *Book of Thought.*

Mercury also corresponds with Wodan/Odin, the Germanic god of wisdom, death, and poetry. This is written into the days of the week, where the English word Wednesday comes from 'Wodan's day', and the equivalent in Spanish is 'Miercoles' (Mercury's day), or 'Mecredi' in French.

The Latin based languages are rooted in the Roman pantheon, whereas English adopted the Norse gods for days of the week, with the notable exception of Saturn.

Day	Monday	Tuesday	Wednesday	Thursday	Friday	Saturday	Sunday
Planet	Moon	Mars	Mercury	Jupiter	Venus	Saturn	Sun
Norse	Mani	Tiu	Wodan/Odin	Thor	Freyja	-	Sunna
Greek	Selene	Ares	Hermes	Zeus	Aphrodite	Kronos	Helios
Roman	Luna	Mars	Mercury	Jupiter	Venus	Saturn	Sol
Spanish	Lunes	Martes	Miercoles	Jueves	Viernes	Sabado	Domingo

Seven days, seven deities.

Hermes may also correspond with the Biblical figure of Enoch, Great-Grandfather of Noah, and author of the apocryphal *Book of Enoch*, one of the occulted texts omitted from the bible (and very much worth reading). The style of writing and the sheer cosmic scale of the subject matters in *Book of Enoch* are uncannily similar to the *Corpus Hermeticum*. Enoch is said to be the Scribe of God, chosen specifically for his wisdom and communicative abilities, to be given the full guided tour of heaven and earth and all that is between and beyond, and to write about it for the enlightenment of generations to come. The divine trio of Hermes, Mercury and Thoth are embodied in the ancient figure of Hermes Trismegistus, a name of Egyptian origin meaning 'thrice great'.

The image overleaf is from Adam McLean's Alchemy Website[1], and is part of a series of paintings depicting the spiritual nature of the seven heavenly rulers, the wandering sky lights, the classical visible planets of Mercury, Mars, Venus, Jupiter, and Saturn, as well as the Sun and Moon. Collectively known as the *Luminaries*, *The Seven*, or *The Septenary*.

[1] Alchemywebsite.com, by Adam McLean

Mercurius.

We see a framed scene of 15th century German city life, lorded over by the father of alchemy, god of merchants and travellers, the cosmic fool and divine messenger himself, Hermes Trismegistus a.k.a Mercurius.

Mercury rules over man's communicative and intellectual faculties, logic and reason, spelling and grammar, creative, entrepreneurial, and alchemical endeavours. The mercurial mind studies nature and produces inspired works of artistic and scientific ingenuity.

Nature is the divine example of perfection and a living message to humanity that the followers of Mercury dutifully translate through creative expression. The beauty of nature is Gods message to humanity, and mercurial souls work tirelessly to deliver it.

Riding high above on a golden chariot driven by Cockerels, Mercurius dressed in scholarly attire, holds a Caduceus staff over his left shoulder. The two wheels of the chariot show the zodiac signs of Virgo and Gemini which are the astrological houses in which Mercury rules.

The Cockerels herald the rising of Mercury on the eastern horizon, as Mercury heralds the coming dawn. The distinctive shrill sound that Cockerels cry out in the pre-dawn hour is nature's wake up call. Mercury commands wakefulness, an alert and receptive mind for God's message to be delivered. Astrologically, we have to be up before dawn at specific times of year to even meet Mercury in the sky, as it always oscillates within 15 degrees of the centre of the solar disc, so visibility is rare.

The people in the courtyard below are diligently and peacefully engaged in collaborative study and creative experimentation; composing music, sculpting, painting, making alchemical potions, doing astrology, trading and socialising merrily. A philosopher's utopia.

Though many will try to denigrate Hermes by calling him 'god of thieves', we don't see any thievery happening in this image, just good honest creative work and the study of nature.

Frequently depicted with winged sandals, a winged staff and a winged hat, Mercurius has achieved three sets of wings, indicating total mastery of the air element. And a nod to the 'thrice-great' of Hermes Trismegistus.

Hendrik Goltzius after Polidoro da Caravaggio, Mercury, (1592)

Chapter 16

The Caducean Connection

The word 'Caduceus' means 'herald's staff/wand' and in Greek mythology it is said that Apollo gave it to Hermes in exchange for inventing the Lyre, the first musical instrument.

From this short story alone, without even looking at the symbol, we can deduce some major insights. Hermes is the inventor of music itself, and the Caduceus represents a reward for musical works, or more generally, a reward for alchemical works, since the crafting of musical instruments from natural raw materials is a form of alchemy.

A Herald is a messenger or envoy, one who can be trusted to convey information accurately, a medium, a prophet, one who announces things to come. Messengers are permitted to travel in all domains of existence, from heaven to hell, since they are a go-between, a courier of divine decree.

The Caduceus symbol is found in a variety of strange places in modern times. It's used by the US army medical corps and is on various world flags and coats of arms. It is sometimes confused with the Rod of Asclepius, the staff with a single snake wound around, used by the AMA and WHO. There is also the 'Nehushtan' or 'Serpent Staff of Moses,' a single bronze serpent wrapped around a staff, forged by God's command, and used to heal the Israelites of serpent bites while roaming in the desert [Num 21:9]. So there are a few early references to a serpent staff with healing powers, but the Caduceus is something more.

Generally it symbolises alchemy by association with Hermes, and since alchemy is about purification, transformation, and medicine, there is a case that the Caduceus is symbolic of healing as well.

The rod represents the spinal column, and the bulbous tip would be the neck and skull. The two snakes represent the energetic channels known as Ida and Pingala. Ida is a Lunar/Yin/Magnetic/Feminine energy, and Pingala is Solar/Yang/Electric/Masculine energy. The two are said to run up and down the spine in a spiral fashion during the process of awakening, represented at the top of the rod by the angel wings.

The snakes are sometimes depicted with 3 points where they cross over, representing the three principles of alchemy, and sometimes also with seven points of crossover, representing the chakras, luminaries, and the seven steps of transformation.

The wings are said to symbolise the virtues of diligence and activity. There is also a strong association with the air element, the mind, freedom. The ability to move freely in all directions, and also an association with angels, the loyal servants of the most high.

The Caduceus can also symbolise the quest for enlightenment through knowledge and wisdom, rising up spiritually through good works and inner alchemy.

Snakes are the lowliest of animals, even lowlier than bugs since they have no legs to keep them off the ground. They shed their skin, symbolic of death and rebirth, and we are told in scripture that they are paradoxically the most wise and cunning of all creatures.

So the serpents are a complex symbol representing intelligence, wisdom and the Kundalini energy, but also deception, wild animal nature, fierce independence and disobedience to God. Serpents are a fiery life force that is unpredictable and notoriously difficult to tame.

In the biblical story, Satan was once a mighty Dragon, beautiful and powerful, Gods greatest creation, but he became so prideful and disobedient that God reduced him to the form of a snake, destined to slither through the dirt until his final judgment at the end of days. The Caduceus depicts the rising up and transformation of consciousness from a lowly state (lead/snake/asleep) to an exalted state (gold/wings/awake). It recognises that we all have this lower devil nature inside of us, and that it must be risen up to meet God so we can be free again.

The Tattoo

In 2017, several years after I began researching Alchemy, I discovered to my surprise that I had a deeply personal connection to this symbol. Almost 10 years earlier in the summer of 2008, after spending an entire week at Boom Festival in Portugal, I returned full of inspiration to create a better life, to devote myself to music and manifest my dreams, and I had a strong vision in my mind.

At the time I described it as "a DNA double helix ribbon with the chakras knitted inside". I don't know where or if I saw it anywhere, but it was a persistent vision that got into my head and stuck with me, I became enamoured with it, drew various interpretations of it, and decided to make it into my first (and only) tattoo.

At this time I was working in an office in Norwich doing technical consultancy for banks, so getting a tattoo on my forearm was a ballsy move, arguably *foolish,* but for reasons of 'soul science' I was determined to do it. Somehow this vision was a gift, and represented my soul's highest aspiration. Getting it made into a tattoo was an act of personal commitment to living an authentic life, pursuing the music career and expressing myself truly.

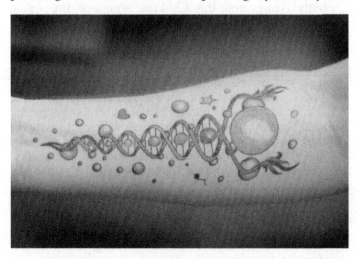

My tattoo, drawn by artist Heather Crowther, inspired by psychedelic vision in August 2008. The 7 central spheres are chakras in the 7 colours of the rainbow.

I saw the DNA helix as representing the Western materialist view of life, where everything is made from atoms and molecules bumping around in space, and the Chakras represent the Eastern spiritual view of life, where everything is seen as energy swirling in the Aether.

This was a 'coincidencia oppositorum', a union of conflicting opposites within me, a conjunction of my western atomic indoctrination with the eastern spiritual knowledge I had gained post-uni.

I made several sketches of the vision and eventually gave them over to an artist to do it properly. Within a few weeks I had a design and proceeded to get it permanently inked onto the underside of my right forearm.

Anyone with a tattoo will tell you, they often end up becoming more meaningful than you could ever have imagined. In 2017, I had a true goosebumps moment when I realised that my tattoo perfectly corresponded with the Caduceus; the twisted strands of DNA were like the twin serpents rising, and the Chakras represent the spinal column. It even had the ribbons opening up and fraying at the top, like the angel wings.

There is also a Star, a Heart, and a Musical Note, as well as some background bubbles for aesthetic effect. The Star is for hope, dreams, ambition and spiritual guidance, while the Heart is for love, home, wisdom and devotion. The Musical Note represents the creative alchemy to which I dedicated myself as a professional and spiritual practice. Recently, I noticed the correspondence that star=fire, heart=earth, music=air and bubbles=water.

So what I thought was a completely original tattoo design born within me from a psychedelic vision, turned out to be the **Staff of Hermes**, an ancient alchemical symbol of transformation and awakening, a reward for good musical works.

At the time of discovering this (2017), I was living on the Big Island of Hawaii teaching Alchemy to music producers. I began to wonder whether I might have some kind of destiny or deeper soul connection to this than I was yet aware of.

Studying the Hermetic teachings daily, I found it all to be highly intuitive, easy, and enjoyable to digest. Everything made perfect sense as if it was simply reminding me of what I already knew long ago.

The writers of ancient alchemical literature seemed to be so pure and eloquent in their words, conferring great wisdom and compassion with every passing sentence. They felt like the words of an old soul mate, a previous version of myself, or some ascended master from beyond the grave. I was struck by how well written and intelligible these 400+ year old writings were, especially when compared to modern academic texts which are so formal, complex, and low-level.

I seemed to be able to remember everything I was reading without any effort. It was as easy as drinking pure fresh water, I could talk about it for days on end without running out of things to say, light bulbs were going on in my head constantly, dots connecting, everything falling into its proper place.

Not everyone may have this kind of enlightenment experience when they first encounter alchemy, and it is likely that I did because of my previous years of study in physics and the shamanic and musical work I had been doing for well over a decade prior. Effectively I had gathered all the pieces together, and alchemy gave me the wisdom to connect it all. It became abundantly clear to me this is the true universal spiritual science that explains all phenomena in real terms, unites all polarities and eliminates all paradoxes.

Alchemy was the enlightenment I had been seeking, I could feel it in my bones. The whole creation started to make perfect sense, illusions were demystified, my eyes were truly opened.

Robert Fludd

In my quest for deeper alchemical knowledge, I discovered a man named Robert Fludd (1574 - 1637), often described as one of the last Renaissance men, a Christian Hermeticist, musician, mathematician, physician and inventor, who produced a staggering amount of original work including a large chunk of classic alchemical literature from this time period.

Fludd attended St John's College Oxford in 1592, where he got a taste for alchemical wisdom in the medical teachings of Paracelsus[1]. In general, what the mainstream refers to as 'Paracelsian medicine' is simply just natural medicine, toxicology. Efforts to heal the body by purification and transformation, rooted in Christian Hermetic philosophy.

Fludd was a big proponent of the Paracelsian approach and an outspoken critic of the 'Galenic' medical system of the time. He graduated with a batcher of arts (BA) in 1596 and had already produced large volumes of work on music

---

[1] Paracelsus: Selected Writings (Bollingen Series Book 139)

and its relation to astrology, then went on to obtain his master of arts (MA) degree before announcing his intention to go travelling abroad.

In his biographical book, *The Greater and Lesser Worlds of Robert Fludd[1]*, we learn that he was one of the first Englishmen to complete his education and go on 'The Grand Tour' of continental Europe. He travelled around meeting people from all walks of life, playing music, teaching, engaging in alchemical experimentation and learning all that he could.

'I have traversed and surveyed with my eyes and mind almost all the provinces of Europe: the surging deep seas, the high mountains and slippery valleys, the crudities of villages, the rudeness of towns and the arrogance of cities' ~ Robert Fludd

By 1605, he had returned to England with the intention of practicing medicine in the Paracelsian tradition. He enrolled at Christ Church College Oxford, and soon ran into trouble as he was unable to contain his disdain and contempt for the established medical paradigm and its practitioners. He was eventually kicked out and stricken off the physician's register. Persistent and determined, he applied to the College of Physicians and was admitted as a candidate in in December of 1607. By March 1608 he was kicked out once more as he 'conducted himself so insolently as to offend everyone'. Eventually in September of 1608, he was accepted again and began his career as general practitioner in London.

The Paracelsian understanding of disease is simply that *'God sends sickness to mankind as punishment for sin ... if we get ill we have none to blame but ourselves, and like Job, we must suffer patiently and prayerfully.'* (referring to Job from the bible).

This is basically the same philosophy as the modern 'health freedom movement', where it is understood that true healing and spiritual growth involves taking responsibility for your condition.

[1] Macrocosm, Microcosm, Medicine, by Jocelyn Godwin

The Temple of Music, by Robert Fludd

"If you examine keenly the parts of the temple, you will be a sharer of all its mysteries and an extremely experienced master in this preeminent knowledge."

Of the Flux

Fludd's body of work is absolutely epic and extensive beyond description. It has to be seen to be believed. He produced hundreds of intricate drawings, designs and inventions, some of which may never have even been made yet.

He was way ahead of his time and it is way beyond the scope of this book to cover Fludd's life work. I hesitate to compare myself to him as he achieved more in one lifetime than I could ever imagine doing, but needless to say I found myself really liking this guy.

Here was someone 400 year ago, who was building self-playing musical instruments, designing perpetual motion machines, documenting the cures for all disease, designing military star-forts, writing treatises on astrology and alchemy, and developing a geocentric model of the cosmos based in musical harmony called the *Monochord*.

He seemed to be into all the same nerdy stuff as me, and his life structure was similar to mine, having gone to university and then went 'on tour' as a musician for many years before returning to his homeland to begin the 'great work'.

As well as his opposition to the medical establishment, he was also a fierce critic of the heliocentric model and the encroaching problem of mathematical theories taking precedent over practical science (the very subject of the first part of this book). He famously had a beef with Johannes Kepler on this issue.

'It is for the vulgar mathematicians to concern themselves with quantitative shadows; the alchemists and Hermetic philosophers, however, comprehend the true core of the natural bodies.'

~ Fludd to Kepler

I couldn't help but feel a strong resonance with Fludd,

and the more I learn about him, the spookier it gets. There were two major synchronicities in 2020 that really brought the goosebumps. Firstly, Robert Fludd was known by the alias *De Fluctibus*, which is a latin term meaning *Of the Flux*, or *Of the Waves*.

My chosen alias since 2003 has been *Hedflux*, a fusion of 'head' and 'flux', describing the state or condition of experiencing visions flowing through the head, like when listening to good music. During these years touring it was not uncommon for people to refer to me as things like 'the flux' or 'flux-head' or 'the fluxmaster' etc. And of course the whole Hedflux project was born *out of the waves.* Electronic music is all about blending and manipulation of waveforms.

I would spend a lot of time making self-playing generative musical instruments on computers, something Fludd was effectively doing 400 years earlier without electricity. I also developed something called Audio Alchemy, a system of musical creativity based in Hermetic teachings and the seven steps of transformation, and Fludd was the only other man I knew of who had done anything even remotely similar to this.

The second big synchronicity came after I had been studying the marvellous work of Marty Leeds[1], a genius polymath, musician, and gnostic preacher who has been working tirelessly to prove the bible is a divinely inspired document, revealing the precise mathematical, astrological and biological correspondence inherent in the words and letters. He has shown that the King James bible is encoded with Gematria using a Septenary cypher, where the letters are all mapped to the numbers 1-7 like so:

A	B	C	D	E	F	G	H	I	J	K	L	M	N	O	P	Q	R	S	T	U	V	W	X	Y	Z
1	2	3	4	5	6	7	6	5	4	3	2	1	1	2	3	4	5	6	7	6	5	4	3	2	1

So every word is reducible to a number, and one number can have many possible words stemming from it.

[1] Pi & The English Alphabet, by Marty Leeds

There is a Gematria calculator at the Gnostic Academy website[1] where you can experiment with words and reveal hidden connections, I highly recommend it.

One day I was inputting names, and I looked to my bookshelf for inspiration, I then typed in the first name I saw which was 'Robert Fludd' for which the numerical value is 48. I perked up in excitement, as I realised this was quite close to the value for my own name 'Steven Young', which is 47.

I briefly felt somewhat deflated as I realised our names are not actually equal, but then I looked again, and perched right next to the Robert Fludd book on the bookshelf, was my very own PhD thesis, and written down the spine was my published author name Steven A. Young.

With my middle initial A (=1) included in the name, it took the total up to 48, and I felt once again goose-bumped at having found another intriguing point of reflection in Robert Fludd. But what does it all mean?

In truth I have no idea what the connection is between us, if any. It could all be just sheer coincidence. I don't claim to be the reincarnation of Fludd, and I doubt I'm related to him, he was high-born and I am a mere muggle. Perhaps we're just two men, 400 years apart, with similar interests and beliefs, a similar alias, similar life pattern and identical name values in gematria.

Maybe it means nothing! Either way, I relish the prospect of diving deeper into the work of Robert Fludd, I have but scratched the surface. He was a genius of unfathomable proportions and has been occulted from history while 'vulgar' mathematical theorists like Kepler, Einstein, and Copernicus got all the glory for their heliocentric sophistry.

---

[1] Gnostic Academy & Church of Lord Jesus Christ, gnosticacademy.org

From the title page of Fludd's treatise *History of the Macrocosm.*

In the image above we see a squatting ape with a schoolmaster's cane, pointing to a book of Arithmetic, the first subject to be covered in the treatise. The ape symbolises *imitation,* it is telling us to '*be nature's ape*', imitate nature by studying it's various fields of knowledge. Going clockwise around the wheel we have; Geometry, Perspective, Painting, Military Science, Mechanics, Timekeeping, Cosmography, Astrology, Geomancy and Music.

In ancient Egypt, the squatting ape was also a symbol of Thoth, the first Hermes, Mercurius the messenger, god of writing, magic, mathematics and alchemy.

Chapter 17

First Stage of The Work

Before an individual can begin to seriously practice alchemy, there are certain psychological, spiritual, and physical requirements that need to be in place and secured. Basic things such as a reliable space in which to operate, access to the elements, a healthy body, a *good wife*, as well as various special tools, materials, instruments and so on.

Besides the mental preparation of unlearning the lies and sophistry with which we have been programmed by the culture of our time, the first stage of the work involves building and securing these fundamental components, for without them one cannot hope to perform even the most basic of experiments.

The alchemist's laboratory is a fractal structure, representing both the practical living and working space of the alchemist, and also his own inner biological laboratory, the house of the soul.

The term 'Laboratory' is a portmanteau of 'Labor' and 'Oratory', meaning 'a place of work and prayer'. In modern parlance a laboratory is generally considered a place for work *only*; a specialised space for scientific labour. It's aesthetically cold, spiritually sterile, nothing whatsoever to do with prayer or God, so is usually abbreviated to just *Lab*. This would be the domain of the chemist, working to supply chemicals to their clients in industry, and more generally any space where secular scientific work is conducted (computer lab, electronics lab).

For the alchemist, however, striving to work under the guidance of nature and divine will, the Oratory is equally as critical as the Lab. Like the shaman and the priest, he utilises the power of prayer in his daily practice, recognising that "no man is great without divine inspiration".

The image is called 'First Stage of the Great Work' from the collection *Amphitheatre of Eternal Wisdom* by Heinrich Khunrath (1617). It is a feast of alchemical gnosis, and a powerful exercise to meditate and decode the many Latin inscriptions and rich symbolism contained within it's etchings.

In the full colour image,[1] the artist makes specific use of the colour green, which can be seen in four key areas. 1) the centre table cloth. 2) the tent on the left. 3) the curtains by the forge on the right. Then 4) way at the back of the room, through the archway with four pillars, in the geometric centre of the circular image, the bed.

Being the middle colour/tone in the octave of visible light, green represents nature and divine neutrality. In each instance, the object in green is a type of cloth. Though we can easily take it for granted in modern times, cloth is sacred, a universal symbol of collaborative work between man and the divine.

Mother Nature supplies the fibre and spinsters spin and weave it into fine and delightful fabrics that give us protection, comfort, dignity, and style. A simple veil of cotton being all that separates our naked flesh from the harsh elements, the thorny bushes or the judging eyes of the world.

Priests are sometimes referred to as 'men of the cloth' for this reason. It represents the veil or boundary between the transcendent domain of divinity - the naked god - and the physical realm of mortal man, a boundary traditionally tended to by clergymen and mystics.

The alchemist goes to church in his own laboratory, every day of the week. Work and worship are one and the same. He seeks union with the divine directly, through prayer, knowledge of scripture, natural law and applied science.

---

[1] The Alchemical Room, by Tommy Westlund
https://alkemiskaakademin.se/The%20Alchemical%20Room.pdf

The Oratory tent on the left contains books of scripture and mathematics and sits right under an impressive library of books along the wall. The Alchemist kneels in wide armed submission to God, humbled to receive the teachings before him.

Music was of fundamental importance to alchemists even in those days, as signified by the musical instruments being placed at the very front and centre of the image nearest the viewer. A violin, lute, harp and mandolin.

Written on the table cloth below it says, '*Sacred Music, defence against sorrow and bad thoughts, because the spirit of God sings with threefold joy in the heart and imbues it with pious affection*'.

Additionally there are bells and shakers and various note pads and stationary tools, weighing scales and little piles of powders indicating the use of dried substances (salts/drugs) for sacrament, healing, or inspiration.

The alchemist's chair is ornate and glorious, like a throne but more comfortable. It is a critical component of the laboratory, the nexus of contemplation. Every artist/alchemist should make the effort to acquire a quality chair. For an alchemist the chair is as important as the bed, being another place where we spend about a third of our lives. Note that the bed, the chair, the table, and musical instruments are all in perfect alignment from the centre down.

The bedroom is the point of convergence of the whole image, the centre of the circle, symbolising how bedroom activities affect every aspect of work and life. How we use our sexual energy affects our character, our karma, and our creativity. The message above the room says 'dormiens vigila,' sleep with vigilance. The bedroom is the inner sanctum where we spend one third of our time resting and regenerating, as well as the place of intimacy, sexual union, and procreation.

The curtained area on the right is the Forge, a rack of ovens, tools, and materials for working with fire. The pillars have inscribed on the base 'ratio' and 'experientia' representing the two hemispheres of the brain and their modes of operation. The left being logical and rational, and the right being intuitive and creative (experiential). The pillars are equal in height indicating the importance of a balanced approach to the work.

Above the Forge, there is a mantelpiece stocked with bottles of potions and various purified substances. The plaque says 'Laboratorium', a place of work and prayer.

The seven spoked candle chandelier on the ceiling represents the seven rays of the luminaries (lumina-rays). Known by many names but most familiar to us as Sun, Moon, Mercury, Mars, Venus, Jupiter, and Saturn, their wandering paths through the sky illuminate and direct the changes that manifest in the human realm on earth.

Many notes are written on the walls and around the room, wise dictums to be kept in front of mind to help the alchemist stay focused on The Work and not fall into dark thoughts, doubt and despair.

- *Without divine inspiration there is no man who is great.*

- *When we attend strictly to our work, God will aid us.*

- *Do not speak of God without light.*

- *That which is wisely tried again will one day succeed.*

- *Sleep with vigilance.*

- *Learn to die well.*

This image is a timeless symbolic instruction manual for alchemists of any generation to develop an inspiring space in which to carry out the work.

Chapter 18

Vessels of Transformation

In practical alchemy there are three vessels nested within one another, that an alchemist requires to perform transmutations:

1. The Laboratory.

2. The Forge.

3. The Crucible.

This can be understood by analogy with the three parts of an egg. The outer hard shell is the brick and mortar walls of the laboratory. The white albumen corresponds to the Forge, being the medium and material fuel for the growth of the chicken. The golden yolk in the centre would be the Crucible, the focal point of heat from the mother hen, the nexus of alchemical transformation.

The Forge is the heart of the laboratory. It is essentially a type of Hearth. A stone cavity where fire is kept and controlled for the purposes of heating, purifying and transforming materials.

There is usually at least one in every house, the heart of the home, the main fireplace, and/or the oven/cooker/ kitchen space.

Home is where the Hearth is, and note the portmanteau of *heart* and *earth.* A home without a hearth is like a soul without a mind, a body without a heart.

The general idea of a hearth is a solid insulated work space with a controllable fire source and a chimney or vent to remove the hot smoke. In the kitchen, this is for purposes of preparing and transforming raw ingredients into delicious meals. Cooking is the most common kind of alchemy we do, the kitchen is like a *homemaker's forge.*

An Alchemist, by Adrian Ostade (1661)

In the painting above, which is in the national gallery, the artist is showing us precisely how *not to be* an alchemist. This is exactly the image of alchemists that sophists would have us believe. Note that the room is a complete disaster, like a bomb has hit it. There is no symmetry, no harmony. The man is madly puffing away at his forge trying to make gold while his wife and child are living in squalor behind him. There is no oratory, no books, nothing inspiring or wise to be found, it is a sad image of desperation and false hope. Don't be like this guy.

Forging a Head

With the advent of distributed electricity, fire-based work was transformed into electrical appliances, and the most common forge people use today is the computer. Here we have a desktop work-horse machine born from the cumulative efforts of engineers, metal workers and smiths. Driven by electricity and capable of storing information and performing rapid calculations, something that was previously only possible in the brains of the most learned human beings.

Elementally, electricity is fire. It's not a separate kind of energy or some exotic stream of particles called 'electrons' or 'positrons', its *fire in the wire*. Copper is a conductor of heat, and we can think of electricity as a 'high frequency heat waves', rapid oscillations in temperature and pressure. At high voltages the oscillations are very dynamic, producing an intense and possibly deadly shock when felt, and like fire it can easily get wild and start blazes if it's out of control.

Electricity is controlled fire, channelled currents of heat energy. It's availability through wall sockets is essentially 'fire on tap', which is how it is used to power kitchens and heat homes instead of more traditional 'wild fire'.

The computer is a forge but also a product of the forge, born of fire and steel. It is said that the first metal tools were the Anvil (a flat pointed lump of metal) and Hammer (a lump of metal on a stick), and these simple devices gave humanity god-like powers to transform the earth.

The gift of understanding how to work with fire and metal is not credited to any one human being. In all cultures this knowledge is understood to have been of divine origin, handed down from above.

The computer and it's many derivative devices (phones and tablets, etc.) are the culmination of centuries of human effort working with fire and metal, gaining ever more precise control over their powers and properties. The handheld computer or smartphone is arguably mans greatest and most powerful creation, and to think it all started with a hammer and anvil.

As God created man in His own image, so man creates technology in *his* own image. The computer is essentially a 'mini-me' representation of man, a robot without arms and legs, a *technological homunculus*.

Applying the principle of correspondence we can see how man and machine share many of the same anatomical parts.

Man	Machine
Eyes	Camera
Ears	Microphone/Keyboard/Mouse/Sensors
Voice	Speakers
Face	Screen
Heart	Power Supply Unit
Brain	Central Processing Unit
Long term Memory	Hard Drive
Short term memory	RAM
Imagination	Graphics card
Language	Computer Code
Organs	Chips
Bones	Motherboard
Skin	Casing
Blood	Electricity
Circulatory System	Wires

Computers speak the language of binary (which was Stephen Hawking's native tongue ... or, native cheek?). All data is reducible to a string of bits, 1s or 0s, on or off, up or down, twitch or no-twitch. Every new bit of information physically alters the state of the tiny metal transistors, flicking the switches, so the machine is constantly reconfiguring itself in response to input and output.

When we are entering data into a computer, typing as

I am now, we are literally transforming metal using fire; the inner fire of our creative will power, the hammering action of our fingers on the keys, the heat buzzing through the circuits and altering the physical state of the metal on the memory chips. It's extraordinary what's really happening when you break it down. It happens so fast that we forget how much is really going on, billions of operations per second.

A laptop full of software, books, and music is worth more than one which is factory fresh, though they both have the exact same weight and technical specifications, the only difference is the data. The memory has been transformed by the installation of software (commands), and now the machine is far more capable, more advanced.

The computer is like the Forge of the Aquarian Age, a personalised fire-driven instrument for boundless creativity, communication, connection, and collaboration, a machine that commands and controls all other machines.

The Crucible

The innermost of the three vessels is the crucible. A container made of ceramic or metal that can withstand the high temperatures of the forge, used for calcination and smelting. The crucible is the focus of the work inside the forge.

In the kitchen there are many crucibles. They are the various pots and pans, cooking dishes, pestle and mortar, double boilers, etc. They hold the substance to be transformed while smoothing out the energy spectrum from the fire, giving a more gentle heat than that of a direct flame. Quite simply, the crucible is where the soup gets cooked, and making metals is a lot like making soup.

In the Audio domain, music is cooked up with a Digital Audio Workstation (DAW), a software package that is installed on the computer to enable musical functions and operations to be performed such as recording, editing, and waveform synthesis. As the computer is to the forge, so the

DAW is to the crucible.

The DAW is where the music hits the metal, where the real creative work takes place, where the magic happens. Waveform data is conducted in real-time through the various circuits and into the loudspeaker coil where every fluctuation of electrical current is coupled to a corresponding movement of the speaker cone. This is where the fire in the wire is converted to sound, a voice, vibrations in the air.

The exact frequency of the voltages in the wire are translated to the air in audible form. In the alchemical sense, sound and light are just different bandwidths of the same vibrational element fire. Sound is not specific to Air, sound travels through Water and Earth as well. Therefore sound is a type of Fire, which is the only element that can penetrate all the other elements.

Software is also a form of fire because it is a set of *commands* for transforming data. Fire is the element of greatest hest, the element with the strongest ability to command the others. It is the prime mover of the three material elements Air, Water and Earth. It penetrates and purifies them. Software is the encoded fire of human will power.

Through raw manipulation of fire and metal on a microscopic scale, these technologies enable ultra precise control of vibration across the whole audible spectrum (and beyond). The modern DAW is an environment where audio can be recorded, generated, sequenced, layered and processed endlessly, providing infinite creative possibilities for music. By extension we can look at any software package as a kind of crucible where precise and specialised commands can be executed, whether for music, coding, graphics, writing, publishing, design etc.

Alchemy isn't just some quaint theory that ran out of steam in the 1800s as sophists would have us believe, it has transformed, broadened, modernised, infiltrated many aspects of life. It is still with us, hidden, obscured, and in some cases right under our noses. We don't recognise it because we are unfamiliar with the ancient teachings, we have forgotten who we really are and what we are capable of.

Chapter 19

The Quintessential Elements

There is profound spiritual wisdom and true scientific knowledge to be gleaned from simply observing and contemplating the nature of the elements. Once again we are speaking of the four classical 'Aristotelian' elements, that correspond with the four states of matter from physics:

- Earth (Solid)

- Water (Liquid)

- Air/Aether (Gas)

- Fire (Light)

The question of whether there are four or five elements is resolved when you realise that Aether, the Quintessence, is essentially Air, and Air is essentially Aether. The Air has many strata of different densities, and Aether is the highest and most pure, the finest grade of Air.

As if by magic, the word 'Aether' is an anagram of 'The Aer', and Aer is the Latin spelling of Air. So for most purposes we will talk of the elements as a group of four, while implicitly understanding that all four elements are born from an omnipresent Air-like substance called Aether.

It feels like a diminishment to call it the 'Fifth Element' (like a fifth wheel) since technically it would be the *first* or even the *zeroth* element, as it is the substance of the space in which all material things manifest. Nevertheless, it is commonly known as the Fifth Element or the Quintessence.

On the surface, the elements are a logical categorisation of the different types of 'stuff' in our human sensory experience, based on universally perceptible qualities of hot, dry, cold, and wet.

Fire is hot-dry

Air is hot-wet

Earth is cold-dry

Water is cold-wet

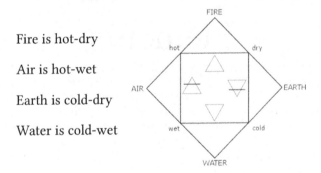

Of course Air can be cool and Water can be hot, the elements can and do mix, but this is the basic configuration of their 'default' properties. It has worked for millennia and was understood by all cultures. Everyone can relate to Fire, Earth, Air and Water. You can literally sense them, you don't need a masters degree to comprehend. Even children and animals can distinguish them.

Though discarded by mainstream science, it is a universal system that is still in use in art and literature and is a key to unlocking the deeper layers of meaning in religious scriptures.

Modern science has distorted the original language of alchemy with ambiguous atomic terminology. The meaning of the term 'Element' was changed during the scientific revolution of the 17th century. It is originally from the Latin Elementum meaning '*a simple and ultimate constituent*'.

The modern definition of 'element' is '*a purified substance consisting only one type of atom*'. This is not only a distortion of the original meaning of the word, it is a full-on inversion that is anchored in atomist ideology.

The periodic table doesn't contain any of the four classical elements. Even Water, once universally understood to be a fundamental constituent of life, is deprived of it's elemental status by this scientific sleight-of-hand. Hydrogen and Oxygen are listed as elements, but Water and Fire are not, however these gases are relatively recent discoveries and largely a product of human labour.

The elements are not chemicals, and the chemicals are not elements.

Elements are the *simple*, ultimate constituents of creation. They manifest as infinitely abundant and freely available resources in their natural state. They can be combined in specific ways to produce 'chemicals'. Remember the word 'chem' means 'black' and symbolises the first stage of al-chem-y, implying all chemicals are products of alchemical transmutation.

Hydrogen and Oxygen are created by running electric current through water in the process of electrolysis. Oxygen is the gas produced at the positive pole (Anode) and Hydrogen at the negative pole (Cathode).

Hydrogen can also be produced by dissolving metals in acid. Acid was known as 'aqua fortis' or 'strong water', and its strength is measured in terms of PH or 'Potential Hydrogen'.

It's important to understand that nobody or nothing is actually creating the water element by smashing hydrogen and oxygen atoms together. Water can't be created, there is a fixed amount of it in the Hermetically sealed realm. If new water were being created then the ocean level would constantly rise, and despite what climate alarmists say, this is not observed.

The notion of 'primary water', made inside the earth by hydrogen and oxygen fusing together, is purely hypothetical and based on atomic-materialist thinking. All water is the same age. It is purified and distilled and revitalised inside mountains, there is no evidence it is created in a chemical reaction. Stagnant water can be filtered and revitalised by letting it flow through earth, or evaporating and condensing, like with clouds and rain.

There is an experiment by Cavendish[1] which is glorified by the scientific establishment and allegedly proves the creation of water from Hydrogen combustion. The experiment is easily reproduced, but the conclusions drawn from it are totally unjustified. When the Hydrogen is ignited it explodes with a loud bang. If you do it inside a bottle, there will be some droplets of water left behind on the glass, and the sophists claim this is proof of an atomic reaction between oxygen and hydrogen to create water. But upon closer examination, the far more convincing explanation is that the droplets are due to condensation from the rapid change in temperature caused by the explosion. Cavendish, and thus all the acolytes of mainstream physics dogma, believe that it shows the water being created by a chemical reaction, but it shows no such thing.

Cavendish is credited as discovering Hydrogen but he wasn't the one who named it. He called it 'inflammable air.' So besides being the only guy to measure gravity and create water in a lab, he is also responsible for making the word 'inflammable' mean the same as 'flammable', something that must have led to much confusion and laboratory calamities in subsequent years.

---

[1] Youtube video 'When Did We Discover that Hydrogen Produces Water When Burned? By BBC Earth Science

The naming of Hydrogen gas was done in the 1770s by Antoine Lavoisier, the 'father of modern chemistry.' It is composed from the Greek 'hydro' (water) and 'genes' (forming, or generating), so Hydrogen is said to mean 'water forming' or 'water generating'.

This is, however, a misleading name predicated on the false claims of the Cavendish work. If, in fact, Cavendish did not create water, then there is no justification in the choice of name, since nobody has actually generated water from 'inflammable air'. But the meaning of the name could be interpreted slightly differently. Instead of 'water generator' it could be 'water generated', since Hydrogen is generated *by* water through application of *fire.*

All purified substances are created by the application of fire, either in the form of heat, light, sound, pressure, electricity or vibration. The idea is to gently simulate the subterranean rhythms deep inside mountains and under the ground, where raw earth is transmuted over time by immense pressures and temperatures into a metal or crystalline gemstone, the way that the coal becomes a diamond.

The various metals, salts, and gasses of the periodic table are not elements, they are the products of transmutation, the fruits of inner earth alchemy.

Some chemicals on the periodic table are not made in the earth at all, but only in the lab. Take the example of Tennessine, atomic number 117, it has a half-life of *50 milliseconds*, meaning that it disappears from existence in the blink of an eye. To call this an element is a lie and a downright inversion of the true meaning of the word. There is nothing elemental about it. It is more like a phantom or a wisp, a momentary energetic event, an *incident*. It literally does not exist.

The periodic table may have some usefulness as a system for identifying chemicals by density (or 'atomic mass'), but let it no longer be called a table of elements, for that it is certainly not.

The true elements are much more relatable, they are bursting with qualities and attributes that flow out from simply contemplating their essential energetic properties, for example:

Earth: solidity, stability, materiality, heaviness, firmness, roughness, inertia, stubbornness, resistance to movement.

Water: fluidity, mutability, receptivity, liquidity, moisture, cleansing, contracting, dissolving, healing, memory, incompressibility.

Air: mobility, lightness, breathiness, swiftness, strength, levity, flight, expansiveness, gustiness.

Fire: light, energy, vibration, transformation, illumination, penetrating, purifying, heating, radiating, electrifying.

The symbols for the elements are divinely simple, communicating their essential behaviour in a universally accessible way.

Earth and Water are denoted by downward pointing triangles, since their tendency is to flow or fall down towards ground level, while Air and Fire are denoted by upward pointing triangles, for their tendency to move up and away from ground.

Fire   Air   Earth   Water

Likewise, in our natural experience of life, the Earth and Water elements are below our feet, but the Air and Fire elements are above in the sky.

The Elements are also gendered. Earth and Water are feminine, receptive, and Fire and Air are masculine, active. The upward triangle is the phallus, and the downward triangle is the womb.

Earth and Water can be held in the hands, but Fire and Air cannot. In physics terms, the feminine elements are what we would call *matter*, and the masculine elements are *energy*.

The word 'matter' relates to *mater, matrix,* and *mother*, because the Earth is our mother, and therefore the Water (which is Mater with an inverted M) is our grand-mother.

From the Hermetic principle of 'As above, so below', we can deduce that The Air/Aether is our father, and the Fire/Light our grand-father.

Man is given life by the 'breath of god' and the 'divine spark', otherwise he is just flesh and blood, an earthen vessel, a corpse.

In scripture, the Holy Spirit is described as a form of Air that is possessed with the will of the father, and enters into people via the breath. People are said to 'fill up' with the Holy Spirit when they are reborn.

Fire   Water   Earth   Air

Element	Qualities	Microcosm (Man)	Macrocosm (Universe)
Fire	Heat, Light, Vibration, Electromagnetism	Soul, Will power, Motive force, Divine spark	The Heavens, the sky, Sun, moon and stars
Air	Gas, Wind, Pressure	Spirit, Thoughts, Intellect, Breath, Communication	Sky, atmosphere, clouds, birds
Water	Liquidity, Density, Depth	Life, emotion, sub-conscious, bodily fluids, blood, sweat, tears, semen	Oceans, Seas, Lakes, Rivers, Fish
Earth	Solidity, Firmness, Inertia	Physical, Bones, tissues, teeth, endurance, stability	Ground, rock, sand, dirt, ore minerals, plants, animals

Here we see the elements by name, their properties and qualities, how they manifest in man (the microcosm), and in the world (macrocosm). This is an application of the Hermetic principle 'as within, so without'.

Diving into the correspondences more deeply, we can pull out many more associations and attributes of the elements.

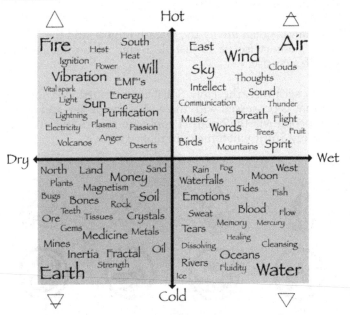

At the boundaries where the elements begin to blend, there are phases of matter that embody mixed qualities such as Fog, which is airy water (or watery air), and Oil, which is an earthy fluid, liquid but not water (oil and water don't mix).

Deserts are sand which is Earth, but they are created by excessive sun which is Fire. Mountains are made of Earth but are also characterised by their great height, which is Airy. Ice is solid like Earth but is also frozen Water.

Earth has inertia; it doesn't move unless acted on persistently by a force. It is also fractal, it has rough edges and looks the same at all scales of magnification (the inspiration for the Mandelbrot fractal).

Water has the property of memory, able to hold thoughts, words, and images in it's interior structure that can be transmitted through drinking or revealed in freezing patterns[1]. It is said that 'water is life', the magnetic fluid of creation. It is capable of receiving all frequencies of light and sound and storing information in it's interior structure.

Power Generation

Electricity in the modern age is sold as a luxury commodity. We pay hundreds of pounds a month to heat our homes. We're told of 'global energy crises' and 'oil reserves running out' and 'rising costs of wholesale energy' etc. We're made to believe it's is this scarce expensive thing while the cost ratchets up every few months in response to world events. But this illusion of the scarcity of energy is 100% conditioned by the parasitic forces behind the energy industry. Add to this the insane 'climate change' hysteria which accuses us of destroying the planet every time we light a wood burner. The truth is that all power/energy/electricity comes from the elements, and it's infinitely abundant. It will never run out.

---

[1] The Secret Intelligence of Water, by Veda Austin. Vedaaustin.com

The table below shows the elements and some of the power generation techniques for each of them, but there are many more ingenious methods:

Fire	Solar cells, concentrated solar power (CSP), Solar thermal plants etc
Air	Windmills, Gas combustion, Atmospheric Electricity, Storm power
Water	Tides, Currents, River Turbines, Waterfalls, Ocean waves, Rain, Steam
Earth	Coal, Wood, Oil, Geothermal, Heat pumps, Magnets, Volcanoes etc

The only reason energy is something scarce and expensive for people is because the energy industry is a racket designed to keep it that way. Energy companies don't make energy, *they make bills*. The so-called 'climate change' narrative is a long running thread of political rhetoric maintained primarily for the purpose of regulating energy and keeping it expensive. In a proper functional nation that isn't riddled with corruption, it needn't cost anything.

A small group of people should be more than capable of satisfying all their energy needs from harnessing the elements at their disposal, but most have no clue how to go about it due to the centralisation of power and the occulting of alchemical knowledge by modern science. One of the first bits of dogma they teach you in high school physics class is, *there's no such thing as free energy*, and it's a big fat lie.

Old buildings often have conical spires with antennas on top, such as we see on churches and cathedrals, and as muggles we are told that it is purely decorative, an aesthetic choice. But with a little scientific knowledge, it becomes apparent that these were for harnessing atmospheric electricity from the aether, though many of them are no longer functioning.

Elements Make Sense

The elements are hard-wired into our human anatomy and the way we perceive the world. We have five physical senses, one corresponding to each:

Sight for Light

Smell for Air

Taste for Water

Touch for Earth

Hearing for Aether[1]

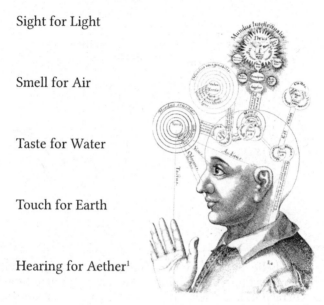

You may be thinking that Hearing is a sense which corresponds with the Air, since we hear sound vibrations in the Air. But in fact, our ears detect vibrations also under Water, and in Earth.

The Ear is the most complex and sensitive instrument we have in our body's laboratory, it detects minuscule pressure changes in all types of medium across a wide bandwidth of frequencies, which we perceive as sound.

The word Aether is also an anagram of '**The Ear**'.

---

[1] Drawing called The Spiritual Brain, by Robert Fludd

Elements at your Fingertips

In the ancient Indian tradition there is the yogic practice of *Mudras,* where the 5 elements are represented on the digits of the hand, like so:

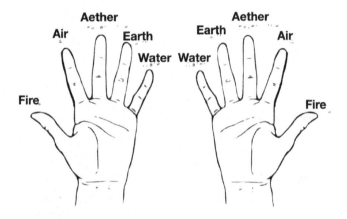

It is believed that by connecting certain fingers with certain other fingers and holding the posture in meditation, the corresponding elements activate within us, altering consciousness in specific ways.

There are hundreds of complex mudras, but the joining of the palms together in prayer is perhaps the simplest. Connecting each digit to its corresponding other, fire to fire, earth to earth, etc.

There are mudras for each of the seven chakras, which by correspondence relates to the seven luminaries and their heavenly attributes. Mudras can be thought of as a way of reconfiguring the antenna of the body to tune into different vibrations of consciousness.

Elements in Food

Alchemy is also cooking. The elements are to be found all throughout our food and medicine and used in the process of food preparation. They also correspond with the different taste groups in both plant and animal kingdom.

Element	Plant	Animal	Taste
Fire	Hot, fiery foods, spice	Red/Game meat	Savoury
Air	Fruits, petals, nectar, flavours, volatile essences	Fowl/Bird meat	Sweet
Earth	Vegetables, seeds, grains, roots, leaves	Animal meat, bugs, insects, "everything that creepeth upon the earth"	Bitter
Water	Seaweeds, Kelp, Watercress, Algae	Fish meat, shellfish, amphibians, waterborne creatures	Salty

"All flesh is not the same flesh: but there is one kind of flesh of men, another flesh of beasts, another of fishes, and another of birds." 1 Cor 15:39

Fire corresponds with heat and red meat. Air with fruits and fowl. Earth with vegetation and 'all that creepeth and crawl'. Water corresponds with fish, seaweed, algae and all the various waterborne creatures.

Fruit is generally to be found high up in the tree, hanging in the Air, while vegetables are found down low, sprouting in or out of the Earth.

There is always mixing of the elements in the various foods, but in general, vegetables are more bitter and less ready to eat than fruit, which is pure sweet perfection. Saltiness is the essential character of ocean based foods, while there is nothing more savoury than flame grilled red meat.

The bible indicates that the elements are living and intelligent aspects of creation. The creatures bear the flesh of the elements. Fish are the flesh of the water, birds the flesh of the air, beasts the flesh of the earth and man, the *flesh of fire*.

What is Wot?

When we look at the etymology of the words we find some even deeper insights. The first thing to notice is that there is a common factor in the names of all the elements, which is '**er**'.

When we sound out the syllables phonetically, we get:

A-er

Fi-er

Wot-er

Er-th

Eth-er

The sound 'er' means 'a repeated action or movement', suggesting the elements are a product of cyclical, wave-like motion. To 'err' is to 'wander, go astray, to make error, to sin'.

According to the christian doctrine we are said to be 'living in sin.' By our very condition, we wander, like the wandering stars, we go astray, we make errors, we miss the mark, it's what we do. Tired of being perfect and blameless, God created man to experience everything else.

Fire is Phi-er, and it is also Pi-er, or Pyre, Pyra, Pyro etc. The use of *Phi* and *Pi* here is no coincidence since Fire is the element of Light, and Light is a vibrational phenomenon described perfectly by the Sine (sin) wave of mathematics.

The constants Pi (3.14..) and Phi (1.618..) emerge from analysis of the **sin** function, and contain all the necessary information for sacred geometry, music, language, technology, and artworks of all kinds. The sinusoidal wave is a fountain of knowledge, the basis of all true physics and applied mathematics.

Light, and thus *Pi* and *Phi*, provide 'illumination', which is what we are seeking. It's also what we are.

When we break down the word 'water', we must first realise that the sound of the word is different from the spelling. Nobody pronounces it *'wat*-er', it's pronounced 'wot-er'. So this begs the question, *what is wot?*

It almost answers itself. Wot means 'to know', 'to see' or 'to receive'. When we wish to know something we say 'wot?' (what?).

Water is the *great receiver*, a liquid antenna that picks up *all frequencies of light, all forms of information.* Water is the *witness* to the Light, it literally SEE'S, that's why it's called *The Sea.*

Our eyes are made from water, our cells are made from water, our blood is made from water, our **seed** is made from water, our body is literally filled with water. The water sees, the water feels, the water speaks, and the water remembers. Water is our emotion.

Water in nature is constantly bathed in the light of the sky, caressed by the currents of the wind. The ocean waves are not caused by the water, they are caused by the air, the waves on the surface reflect the action of the winds. Sunlight (*phi-er*) has a potent cleansing effect on water, which is why tropical regions have such perfect turquoise blue waters rich in colourful displays of aquatic life.

Aether & Hydrogen

The blue hue we see in the clear sky and tropical waters is said to be a perceptual characteristic of Aether. Blue sky is only seen on clear days. It is not observed under the clouds or at low altitudes. The blueness is coming from very high up, above the highest cloud layer and the height of aircraft and drones.

Only the most purified water is capable of reflecting the Cerulean Blue of the Aether. Cerulean is defined as the specific shade of blue of the clear sky at the azimuth, directly over your head, at the moment of dawn, when the sun peaks over the horizon.

Aether we know is a type of Air. It means 'upper air, heavenly air, bright air', a source of pure potential, the 'breath of the gods.' If we accept the notion of the Hermetically sealed realm, we would expect the higher parts of the dome to be rich in Hydrogen and Helium. Being less dense than air, they 'defy gravity,' move rapidly upward and never seem to come back down. It stands to reason they would be concentrated in the canopy. Aether could well consist of these 'lighter than air' gases, the first two entries on the periodic table.

Atomic science declares that 'all atoms are made from Hydrogen', since it is said to be the smallest and most basic unit of thing. Since we know 'Hydrogen' is a misleading 17th century name contrived from an easily debunkable Cavendish theory, it may be safe to presume that what we call Hydrogen is actually Aether, or the closest thing to it.

The prefix Aeth- or eth- in chemistry means 'two', so this tells us Aether is something containing a twoness, both genders, something with positive and negative attributes. Aether with an 'A' refers to the ancient greek concept of the quintessence, whereas Ether without the 'A' refers to a class of chemical solvents.

Hydrogen is said to have one electron (negative/lunar pole) and one proton (a positive/solar pole), the simplest dynamic electrical system there is. Furthermore, when Hydrogen is ignited it produces a pale blue flame, which is barely even perceptible in daylight conditions.

Hydrogen + Fire = the colour of a clear blue sky.

Aether as Heavenly Father

The balanced interplay of masculine (+ve) and feminine (-ve) polarities are necessary for the creation of anything, so Aether represents that perfect everlasting unity of the genders that is the precursor to all of creation.

Though technically gender neutral, the Aether is symbolic of the 'Father of the gods', the God preceding all other gods, 'the most high', the Almighty, the element that gives rise to all other elements.

High-drogen is literally the *most high Air*, since it is the least dense and most pure and simple. It looks down on us from up on high. Hydrogen rushes up toward heaven the moment it is released from matter. It must be captured and trapped in upside-down bottles in order to be utilised down here on the earth plane.

Recreational drugs are high in Hydrogen content, and they get you 'high', leading to many sincere testimonials of ecstatic bliss and encounters with God. Could this be caused by the sensation of Hydrogen releasing from the drug-salts, rising up through the blood stream and into the brain?

Jesus Christ is called 'the risen one', the *son* of the Father/Aether. Helium, named after Helios the sun god, is another rising gas that is the *son of Hydrogen*, and said to be produced by ... *the Sun!*

In Scottish language, Father is pronounced as *Faether*, which contains the whole word 'aether' within it. It sounds like *faither*, as in one who provides faith, or the one in whom we have faith.

'Aether' can be transposed and anagrammed into many other related terms such as; the aer, the ear, earth, heart, hearth, theatre, weather, the area, heater, and 'a three' (from the twoness comes a three).

Elemental Surnames

The convention of mandatory family names or surnames is said to have been established gradually between the 11th and 14th century in Europe and the UK. There are generally four types of surname. Whenever we see a group of four properties, we can almost always find the correspondence to the elements, since they are the most fundamental 'foursome' in creation.

Patriarchal (Fire);

> Named after the father e.g. Stevens (female), Stevenson (male), Richards, Richardson, etc.

Occupational (Air);

> Named after the function/skill e.g. Taylor, Butcher, Baker, Shearer, Skinner, Smith, Potter, Fisher, Farmer, Barber, Clark.

Locational (Earth);

> Named after the dwelling place, or a characteristic thereof, e.g. Newport, Townsend, Greenhill, Burnside, Atwood, Forrest, etc.

Relational (Water);

> Named after a distinctive trait, quality or feature, or a nick name; e.g. Young, Youngman, Oldman, Large, Small, Long, Hardy, White, Brown, Grey (referring to hair colour, not skin colour).

We could also even define a fifth category of surname corresponding to the Aether, which would be *chosen names.*

For most of us, names are *given* at birth by someone else and surnames are inherited by formality. Though our father or grandfather may be have been a 'Skinner' doesn't necessarily mean that we or our sons and daughters will continue to work the trade of skinning animals. At some point people may wish to choose a new family name, based on whatever combination of elements they wish, and many people do.

Death Rites

The elements also correspond with the death procedures available to us at the end of life:

Element	Death Rite	Process	Description
Fire	Cremation	Calcination	Reduced to Ashes
Water	Burial at Sea	Dissolution	Eaten by Fish
Earth	Burial in the ground	Putrefaction	Eaten by Worms
Air	Desiccated/Donated	Separation	Carved into pieces by medical students, thrown into biohazard waste bins, or ground up and made into drugs

There was a time when I thought donating to science was the way to go, but given what I've learned about the medical industry in recent years I'd rather get eaten by worms or fishes. There is some appeal in cremation, fire is the cleanest element, and the other three seem like very long-winded ways of getting to the same result, reduced to mineral salts and scattered in nature. Also being cremated ensures that the body can't be reanimated by a necromancer or caught up in some future zombie apocalypse.

The question of what to do with the ashes it not something I wish to explore here, but there is a variety of occult alchemical operations that can be done with them. In some places alchemists would get buried with metal cages around their graves to prevent people from stealing parts of their corpse, which could be used to capture something of the essence of the deceased individual.

191   *The Secret Art of Alchemy*

The Elemental World

The image below is part of a larger emblematic piece by Johann Daniel Mylius (1619), the title *Mundus Elementaris* means The Elemental World.

There is a treasure trove of alchemical wisdom encoded in this piece. I recommend getting stuck into it, decoding and translating all the latin, make the correspondences for yourself[1].

It relates the elements, zodiac and seven luminaries to their corresponding metals, organs of the body, and archangels. In the inner circles we see twelve fields of knowledge, grammar, dialectics, rhetoric, music, physics, astronomy, arithmetic, geometry, medicine, jurisprudence, theology, and **alchemy**.

---

[1] Wonderfully coloured version at www.topfoto.co.uk/asset/2516388/

Chapter 20

The Tria Prima

One of the most powerful concepts for understanding Alchemy, is the Tetractys of Pythagoras, a simple visualisation of the numbers 1-4 which hides within itself the core of all spiritual and scientific knowledge.

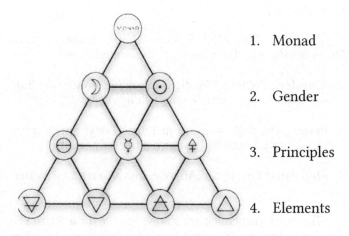

1. Monad

2. Gender

3. Principles

4. Elements

If we take knowledge as consisting of symbols, and those symbols being ultimately reducible to numbers (A=1, B=2, etc), then we can view all knowledge as a pyramidal structure, emanating from the first and most influential of all numbers; 1,2,3, and 4, the capstone of knowledge.

There is no knowledge without these numbers. They are the foundation and source of everything that can be known or manifested. Their importance cannot be overstated. All the other numbers, 5-9, can be created by combinations of these first four.

We also have, 1+2+3+4=10, the number of digits on our hands and feet, and 1x2x3x4=24, the number of hours in the day.

Ten (10) represents fullness and completion, the perfect wholeness of unity next to the infinite emptiness of zero, the beginning and the end in conjunction. This is why 10 is the basis for the number system. Ten marks the moment of reset from 9 back to 0. Nine is the highest pure number, 1 is the lowest.

Each number of dots in a row relates to a fundamental concept in Alchemy. They are highly symbolic and their meaning can be illuminated with key correspondences. For example:

1. **The One.** The Monad, God, Unity, Aether, Source, Universe, the All, the most high, the Almighty etc ...

2. **Gender.** Polarity, duality, inflow/outflow, +/-, Sun/Moon, male/female, man/woman, king/queen etc.

3. **Principles.** Salt, sulphur, mercury; body, mind, spirit; cardinal, fixed, mutable; tria prima; the holy trinity

4. **Elements.** Fire/Ignis, Air/Aer, Earth/Terra and Water/Aqua.

The three principles are known as the **Tria Prima** or the Three Primes, a sacred trio with relevance in many different fields of knowledge.

In Alchemy they are commonly represented by Sulphur, Salt and Mercury. All the elements are symbolised with triangles which points to a triplicity inherent in their fundamental nature. As with the elements, we can derive meaning from simply contemplating the properties and qualities of these materials.

Salt

This principle represents structure, stabilising, enduring, persevering. It is associated with coagulation, grounding, and physicality. The principle of salt is beyond just food flavouring, it represents coarse, dry matter, fixedness, resistance to change. Salt preserves, it prevents decay and putrefaction. It is symbolically associated with the colour black, corresponding to the Nigredo or 'blackening', which purifies a substance with Fire until there is nothing left but the unburnt, immortal, irreducible Salt.

Mercury

Also known as 'quick silver' or 'the water that doesn't wet the hands', the principle of Mercury represents the passive and receptive element in Alchemy, the universal solvent, the mind. It is associated with fluidity, conductivity, adaptability and the unity of opposites (metallic and liquid, watery, but not wet, active yet passive). Mercury is highly sensitive to fire, expanding or contracting in direct proportion to the ambient temperature. The principle of mercury is often symbolised by a hermaphrodite or a serpent. It is associated with the colour white, in correspondence with 'the Albedo' or 'the whitening'.

Sulphur

Also known as 'brimstone', 'stone of fire' or 'soul of fire' (soul-fire), represents the energy in matter, the solar principle in raw material form, a fusion of fire and earth. It is associated with transformation, purification, and the release of energy. A key component in explosives and corrosives, the principle of sulphur is often symbolised by a Dragon or a Lion in Alchemical art, it is yellow-gold colour in appearance, and is associated with the Citrinatas (yellowing) and Rubedo (reddening), the final stage of the work when the spirit is infused into matter.

In Herbal Alchemy, Sulphur corresponds with Oil, and Mercury with Spirit (liquor/alcohol). All plant material can be reduced and separated into these three principle components:

Principle	Being	Correspondence	Process
Mercury	Spirit	Liquor/Alcohol	The volatile liquid obtained from fermentation and distillation of the material
Sulphur	Soul	Essential Oil	The viscous essence remaining after removing all water-soluble material
Salt	Body	Mineral Powder	The dried powder remaining after calcinating the raw material

The art of separating plant materials into these component parts and recombining them is called **Spagyrics**.

The term comes from the Greek "spao" (separate) and "ageiro" (combine), and refers to the process of isolating and purifying the principle components, then recombining them to create a potent and balanced healing remedy containing the body, spirit, and soul of the plant. Common supplements available in the 'drug stores' are at best only the Salt/Body of the plant, and usually defiled with unnatural additives.

In Spagyrics, the plant is viewed as a complete system, and the goal is to extract and preserve all of its essential components, the physical (salt), energetic (oil), and spiritual (liquor) properties, in order to create a medicine that is far more concentrated and effective than any one individual part, and greatly superior to taking the plant in it's raw form.

The Three Primes manifest in life as Body, Soul, Spirit,

the three-fold structure of man, the microcosm. Spirit is the sustenance of the Soul, and the Body is its temple. Upon death the Soul is released back to the Aether.

This idea of a unified 3-in-1 triune is found in many traditions, and symbolised by the Borromean rings:

Named after the Italian aristocratic family Borromeo, whose coat of arms bears the symbol, it is a set of three interlocking rings that are arranged in such a way that if any one of the rings were to be removed, the other two would also come apart. Such an arrangement is also known as a Trinity.

There are many sacred trinities that form the core principles of different fields of knowledge, and with the tria prima we can make correspondences between the 3-fold structure of man and the 3-fold structure of divinity.

The Father corresponds to the Soul, the droplet of divine likeness inside each of us. The son Jesus (or Adam) corresponds to the Body, flesh and blood, 'the temple not built by human hands'. The Holy Spirit is the Great Spirit, Wakan Tanka, the power of God in the Air, the receiver of prayers, source of breath and all true inspiration.

The Body corresponds to Adam, the first man, and Jesus, sometimes called 'the second Adam', who are described as real flesh & blood humans like us. They carried within them the soul of God and were 'full of the holy spirit'.

Body	Jesus, Adam, Son	Physical vessel of flesh and blood, mortal man of earth
Soul	Christ, The Father	Eternal, transcendent principle, immortal above
Spirit	Holy Spirit	Consciousness, powers of the Air, the great sky

Though this ancient wisdom is often criticised for being too 'patriarchal', it applies equally well on the feminine side, via the principle of polarity and 'as above, so below':

Body	Mary, Eve, Daughter	Physical vessels of flesh and blood, mortal woman of earth
Soul	Gaia, Mother Nature	Eternal, transcendent principle, immortal below
Spirit	Sacred Waters	Subconscious, powers of water, the great deep

There is a mirror symmetry between masculine Air and feminine Water, they are both fluid, and can carry currents of energy and move together.

If the spirit of the Father acts in the Air, then the spirit of the Mother acts in the Waters, this follows from the Hermetic principle of As Above, So Below.

One of the opening lines in the Old Testament, Genesis 1:2 reads: "*And the earth was without form, and void; and darkness was upon the face of the deep. And the Spirit of God moved upon the face of the waters.*"

The image is of a time before creation, when all that existed was Aether above Water, and the spirit of God is described as a movement on the waters surface (surface means 'over face', so this implies that the water has a face that faces *up*).

The surface of the water is a horizontal plane of interaction where waves of all sizes oscillate back and forth, Air against Water and Water against Air. It is a very thin and specialised state of matter that is uniquely sensitive to all frequencies of vibration, a perfect mirror when still, and also an antenna of infinite bandwidth. It is in this layer of tension between 'the above' and 'the below' that God, life and light found its initiatory spark.

Astrological Modes

In Astrology, the Tria Prima is expressed as the elemental modes; Cardinal, Fixed and Mutable, which are the different behaviours or operating characteristics of the elements.

1. Cardinal - leading, initiatory, positive, masculine, fiery.

2. Fixed - unchanging, stable, structured, grounded, earthy.

3. Mutable - changeable, receptive, negative, feminine, watery.

Three modes times four elements gives twelve elemental actions, which correspond with the twelve signs of the Zodiac:

1. Aries - Cardinal Fire

2. Taurus - Fixed Earth

3. Gemini - Mutable Air

4. Cancer - Cardinal Water

5. Leo - Fixed Fire

6. Virgo - Mutable Earth

7. Libra - Cardinal Air

The Secret Art of Alchemy

8.   Scorpio - Fixed Water

9.   Sagittarius - Mutable Fire

10.   Capricorn - Cardinal Earth

11.   Aquarius - Fixed Air

12.   Pisces - Mutable Water

Zodiacal signs are composed of an element and a mode. With this knowledge we can observe nature and identify examples where these specific elemental actions take place:

Action	In Nature	Ruler
Cardinal Fire	Sparks, Friction, Lightning, Ignition, Abrasion, Ramming, Volcanos; the starting impulse	Mars
Cardinal Water	Rain, Springs, Streams, Rivers, Tides, Fountains; living water	Moon
Cardinal Air	Winds, Storms, Gusts, Gales, Tornado; strong changes in pressure	Venus
Cardinal Earth	Lava, Wood, Crystals, Ice; growing, forming, materialising earth	Saturn
Fixed Fire	The Sun, the sacred fire, the hearth; always burning and shining	Sun
Fixed Water	Contained, stagnant or trapped water; lakes, bogs, swamps, acids, poisons, gels, pastes etc	Mars
Fixed Air	Gases, Aether/Hydrogen, Steam, clouds, Oxygen, Argon, Nitrogen; the Air we breath	Saturn
Fixed Earth	Rock, stone, gems, precious metal; earth that resists and persists	Venus
Mutable Fire	Light frequencies, EMF, Electricity, Magnetism	Jupiter
Mutable Water	Volatile liquids, spirits, solvents	Jupiter
Mutable Air	Sound, audible vibrations; the powers of the air	Mercury
Mutable Earth	Soil, Oil, Sand, Clay and Dust; flowing, malleable earth	Mercury

In this way, we can see how the principle of 'As above, so below' comes into play, as the elemental properties of the zodiacal signs correspond with physical substances and process domains in the earth realm.

Through the system of astrological rulership, deeper connections are revealed. For example the Moon rules Cancer which is Cardinal Water, so we see how the moon rules over rivers, tides and springs and so on.

The sun and moon each rule one house, while the other five planets rule two each. The Sun rules Leo, which is Fixed Fire, the prime source of heat and illumination. The hottest month of the year in the north, also known as 'the dog days of summer'. The Sun rules over summer and the hour of noon, its highest point in the day time sky.

Mars (the roman god of war) rules Aries (Ares is the greek god of war), which is the spring time. Thus Mars/Ares is a leader, a fire starter, an antagoniser, creating sparks, friction and tension, igniting conflicts, and blazing trails. Mars also rules over Scorpio, fixed water, which is symbolised by one of the most intimidating, well armed and deadly creatures in all of creation. It carries a sack of poison in it's tail, which is the 'fixed water' it uses to kill its prey.

Mercury rules over Gemini and Virgo, Mutable Air and Mutable Earth, these are the domains of communication, purification and transformation, language, art, science, knowledge, alchemy, industrious and creative activities.

Mutable Earth like clay is used for building and construction, fashioning bricks to make homes, as well as having a purifying effect on the body, extracting toxins when applied to the skin. Mutable Earth is like amalgam or putty, flexible in form, endless utility.

Venus, associated with beauty and fertility, rules Taurus which is Fixed Earth, precious gems and metals, fine aesthetics, statues, wealth, stability and security. Also Libra, Cardinal Air, the winds of change, storm power, justice, judgement, the restoration of balance. Avoidance of extremes.

Jupiter rules Sagittarius and Pisces, Mutable Fire and Mutable Water, electricity, power, beneficent technologies, high society, religion, dreams, fantasies and ambition.

Saturn is the only planet to rule two consecutive signs, Capricorn (Cardinal Earth) and Aquarius (Fixed Air), and so has a particularly long period of action when traversing those signs. As the slowest moving of the seven luminaries, it corresponds with Lava, Wood and Crystals, the slow growing cardinal aspects of earth, where new land-forms are created gradually over long periods of time.

Venus	Jupiter	Sun	Mars	Moon	Mercury	Saturn
Copper	Tin	Gold	Iron	Silver	Quicsilver	Lead

Atomic Correspondence

In Atomic theory, the tria prima manifests as the sub-atomic triad, the proton, electron, and neutron, which are said to constitute all matter. The table below shows the correspondence:

Body	Soul	Spirit
Salt	Sulphur	Mercury
Fixed	Cardinal	Mutable
Electron	Proton	Neutron
Negative / Inward	Positive / Outward	Neutral
Feminine Principle	Masculine Principle	Hermaphrodite

With this we can start to understand that when the physics student says 'everything is made from protons, neutrons and electrons,' it is really a distant echo of the alchemists saying 'everything is made from salt, sulphur and mercury', or the mystic who says that 'everything has a body, spirit, and soul.'

We can also start to see where atomic theory got much of its ideas from, by taking timeless alchemical and religious principles and inverting them. The electron is a reification of the feminine principle of inward flow, and the proton is masculine or outward flow.

The celebrity theorist Michio Kaku has all but admitted that quantum physics is rooted in 'Jewish Mysticism' and the teachings of the Zohar. This could also help explain the preponderance of Jewish idols in theoretical physics.

Curiously, all equations in quantum physics revolve around a minuscule number known as *Planck's Constant*, which is denoted by the symbol '$\hbar$', called "h-bar", the alchemical symbol for Saturn. It breaks down into a cross, symbolising matter, with a lunar crescent below, symbolising mind. Thus, it represents the principle of *matter over mind*, which is *materialism.*

Chapter 21

The Alchemical Wedding

'The grandest ambition that any man can possibly have, is to so live, and so improve himself in heart and brain, as to be worthy of the love of some splendid woman; and the grandest ambition of any girl is to make herself worthy of the love and adoration of some magnificent man. There is no success in life without love and marriage. You had better be the emperor of one loving and tender heart, and she the empress of yours, than to be king of the world. The man who has really won the love of one good woman in this world, I do not care if he dies in the ditch a beggar, his life has been a success.' ~ Robert Ingersoll

The Alchemical Wedding is a perfect union of energetic opposites represented by the 'Marriage of the Sun and Moon', a conjunction, or solar eclipse.

It is a little known fact that the tradition of marriage is itself based in the alchemical wedding. It is a commitment to the Great Work of devoted love to another, to share in the spiritual journey of life 'till death do us part.' It is an acknowledgment of man and woman as two equal and necessary halves of the divine, a loving union of body, spirit, and soul.

The wedding ring is symbolic of the ring of fire that occurs during an eclipse, when the Sun and Moon are conjunct in the sky.

At the moment of totality the sun and moon form a **golden ring**. Gold metal is the coagulated fire of the Sun, and the golden ring is placed on the 'Annular finger', which corresponds with the element of Earth, and on the left side, which is feminine/lunar.

Thus the wearing of the ring is a unification of the powers of the Sun and the Moon, the Above and Below, the Fire and the Earth, the Masculine and Feminine; an Alchemical Wedding.

We can understand now why the world seeks to cheapen, diminish, and tarnish marriage, making it out to be a pointless religious ritual or just a legal contract between two cohabitant citizens. People say marriage is 'just a piece of paper' or a 'ball and chain', but it's original meaning and significance is something much more sacred, *marriage is high alchemy.*

Blaspheming marriage is part and parcel of the same age-old war against God, an attack on families and love itself. An effort to hide the true science of alchemy, to obfuscate the great work, and usher in a dystopian communist panopticon of atomised individuals ruled by demonic overlords.

In alchemical lore, the marriage is sometimes represented in abstract form as a hermaphroditic icon known as Rebis, in which both masculine and feminine polarities are overtly joined together.

In the image, the Rebis has two heads, one solar-masculine on the right and one lunar-feminine on the left. In one hand there is a compass and another is the square symbolising the 'squaring of the circle' and the unity of the two geometric genders of the line and the curve.

As well as the Sun and Moon, the energy of Venus (♀) and Mars (♂) are united, as are Jupiter (♃) and Saturn (♄), while Mercury (☿) shines directly overhead.

Standing on a great fire-breathing Dragon represents the triumph of the human spirit over all the evils, temptations and distractions which befall us. It is a sign of having conquered fears, overcome adversity, completed the inner work against all odds and tamed the desires of the lower animal nature.

The Rebis and Dragon are stood on a 2-winged ruby red stone that is etched with the digits 4 and 3 on a square and triangle, respectively. The numbers are of great significance in alchemy, representing the elements, the principles, and by extension 4+3=7, the steps of transformation, chakras, and luminaries.

The winged object represents the Philosopher's Stone itself, the most precious material in alchemy, carefully crafted by collaboration of man and God, said to be able to transmute Lead into Gold, cure all disease and extend life.

The Sun and Moon are the heavenly exemplars of the gender polarity, the King and Queen of the Sky, equal in magnitude, opposite in effect. One ruling over day and one ruling over night. They have always been gendered due to their essential energetic relationship. They operate like poles of a battery.

Gender is fundamentally about energy flow; the sun is masculine due to it being an outflow of energy, while the moon is feminine for being an inflow of energy.

The Sun operates by way of heat, while the Moon operates by way of cold. The Moon light is measurably colder than the night shade, it does not reflect the Suns warmth, as we're told. The moon is not radiating or reflecting the sun. We can look directly at it without eye damage, it does not illuminate the sky around it.

Radiation, the outflow of energy, is masculine or positive. Absorption, the inflow of energy, is feminine or negative.

In Latin languages the Sun and Moon have gendered names, El Sol, and La Luna. In many non-english languages, all the nouns are gendered, which reveals the essential energetic character of the object being discussed, and affects how its name is used in sentences.

The English language has omitted gendered nouns for some reason, though they are used within all the other languages English is based on (Germanic, Norse, French, Latin).

To an English speaking person, the very notion of the Moon being feminine is bizarre and unhinged (how can it be feminine? It's just a ball-shaped rock floating in outer space!!?). Even the Sun being masculine is weird, though to a lesser extent, since 'sun' is homophonic with 'son.' But masculinity is typically something only associated with people or animals, not objects.

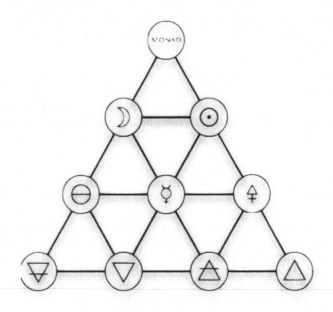

The tetractys with alchemical symbols in place shows the hierarchy of emanations from the singular godhead a.k.a the monad or aether. The first division is into the sun and moon, the two genders, and opposing poles necessary for the creation of any dynamic system.

Then come the three primes. Note how salt ⊖ is on the feminine side under moon ☽, and sulphur ♄ on the masculine side under sun ☉, but mercury ☿, being hermaphroditic, is bang in the middle.

The two feminine elements water and earth then follow from the salt and mercury. The two masculine elements, air and fire, follow from mercury and sulphur.

The male-female gender polarity is sometimes expressed as 'fixed' and 'volatile'. The Sun is energetically fixed, though it rises and sets locally, its timing is flawless, you can set your watch by it. It never ceases radiating fire in it's path. If you followed the sun you could stay in daylight forever. It's always daylight somewhere. In northern parts of Alaska inside the Arctic circle, the sun doesn't set for 82 days between May and August, it just goes around and around the sky in a wiggly wave (known as the 'midnight sun').

Conversely, the moon is volatile, it has phases, changing in power and brightness, disappearing from the sky completely for 2+ days of the month, only to be reborn anew. The timing of the lunar cycles is irrational, it cannot be expressed as a whole number of hours or days, thus it is always forming new aspects with the Sun. The moon has an intrinsic cycle of growth and decay while the sun shines continuously, changing in quality only as it traverses through the zodiac on the line of the ecliptic.

The sun corresponds with fixed fire (Leo) and the moon with cardinal water (Cancer). When the sun is at it's highest point in the sky, this is high noon, peak light. When the moon is at it's highest point in the sky, this is high tide, peak water. When high tide and high noon coincide, the waters are at their most clear and deep.

The moon lifts the salt water by paramagnetic attraction, while the angle of the sun determines the warmth and clarity of the waters (equatorial regions have bluer waters and lesser tide swings). There's no 'gravity' involved, it's moving by electromagnetism and pressure waves in the aether. The Sun exerts a magnetic influence on the water as well, though it's only about 40% as strong as the moons influence, the moon dominates the water.

Fire and Air correspond with the whole sky, the source of light itself, even dark patches of sky are gleaming with light, and the Air is above and all around and inside of us. Indigenous wisdom universally recognises this as **Father Sky**.

Earth and Water correspond with the rivers, oceans and ground of our being, **Mother Earth**, the plants and animals, the great natural world and all that holds us together, our bones, tissue, muscles and blood.

In the Greek tradition Uranus is the Sky Father (air+fire), and Gaia is the Earth Mother (water+earth). The sexual union of these elemental gods takes place at the surface of the earth, and this mixing of the masculine and feminine elements produces the miracle we call life.

We are all children of Father Sky and Mother Earth.

The gender of the elements is encoded in the design of the symbols, with the upward triangle representing the masculine phallus, while the downward triangle represents the womb/uterus.

Joining them in a balanced union produces the six pointed star, a symbol of Aether which is gender balanced, a perfect combination of two opposing trinities, male and female.

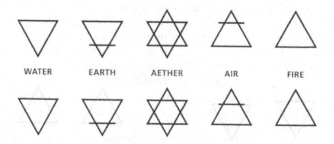

WATER   EARTH   AETHER   AIR   FIRE

Be aware that the alchemical symbols such as the six pointed star and the caduceus are ancient, *as ancient as can be*, and that over the centuries certain human tribes have appropriated them for coats of arms, flags and corporate emblems, even distorting the original meaning or claiming ownership.

Gender is a major target of the well-poisoners at the time of writing this. Social engineers are 'inventing genders' and new 'pronouns' all the time and peddling them to gullible screen-agers as sexual diversity. One can't help but wonder if this is partly a consequence of the absence of gendered nouns in the English language, or perhaps it is a 'mind virus' such as *Wetiko*.

Languages with gendered nouns are called *romantic*, and for an English speaking person learning say, French or Spanish, it is noticeable how much more sexy and flirty it sounds than what we are accustomed to. English is notoriously unromantic, unsexy. It's a case of 'no sex please we're British.' Literally, gender has been eliminated from the language at the root level. This makes it quite useful as the language of science and commerce, but not great for romance and reproduction.

Consider the Spanish national dance, Flamenco. It is highly sexually charged and dynamic, and leaves couples eager to go home and make babies all night long. On the other hand, English Morris dancing is perhaps the most lame and unsexiest of all national dances, just a bunch of crusty old men skipping around with hankies.

Gender is synonymous with the number two, it's the cosmic twoness. If there is any case is to be made for a third gender, then it can only be neutral, the middle point, the androgyne or hermaphrodite, the balance of all masculine and feminine polarities, the sum of the genders.

But technically neutral is not a gender just as zero is not a number, because gender is about direction of energy flow. In a marriage, there is both the man and the woman, it is the balanced combination of the two, sometimes called the 'bridegroom', a *natural* and *unified* whole with both genders together as one.

Energy flows in two ways: outward or inward, clockwise or anti-clockwise. When energy flows outward or clockwise this is called positive or masculine, when it's inward or anti-clockwise, this is called negative or feminine. There are no moral attributes here, negative is not worse than positive, it's just the opposite direction of flow. Both directions are necessary for anything to be happening at all.

The gender difference between men and women relates to the reproductive process where the man's role is an outflow or giving of energy (semen) and the woman's role is an inflow or receiving of energy (egg), as well as hosting the gestation and growth of the child within herself (woman = womb-man).

This polarity only applies to the reproductive process however. There are many masculine and feminine processes occurring within all people all the time. For example, talking is a masculine process (outflow) while listening is feminine (inflow).

The mouth itself is feminine, but nipples are masculine. It's all about the direction the energy flows.

In an electrical circuit or plug, the positive terminal is masculine and is inserted into the negative terminal which is feminine. I don't wish to cause arousal or awaken the snake, so needn't be anymore descriptive than this about the basic binary mechanics of gender, suffice to say the union of masculine and feminine poles is necessary for the creation of life, for electrical or magnetic action to work, and it is also essential for creation of good art.

Consider the potter; clay is feminine as it is made from earth and water, the feminine elements, and it receives shape and form by the forces of the Potter's fingers, pushing and prodding and sculpting with intent and skill. This is the masculine side of the process. The repeated penetration of the fingers into the feminine clay is a form of sexual union, a labour of love that ultimately gives birth to the clay pot.

To make art is to make love to the medium. For the musician, playing music is a masculine process, an outflow of movement, harmonic sound and rhythm, while the audience listening and dancing is feminine, receiving the frequencies and vibrations.

It can be man or woman, it doesn't matter, but the inherent gender of all objects and processes is something of profound importance that has been eliminated from our language, and it appears to have had dire consequences on the sexual health of the culture at large.

It should be common knowledge that all good things are produced by the union of masculine and feminine components, it is obvious when one observes the behaviour of nature. Instead this is hidden, obfuscated and mocked.

Romance in language is important, it produces *chemistry* which is the precursor to creation. Life on all levels is the product of 'sexual chemistry', the 'alchemical wedding' or as the magicians like to call it 'sex magic'. New things are born when energetic opposites come together and *dance.*

The mathematical representation of sex is two becoming three, mother plus father becomes mother, father, and child. The word 'sex' is homophonic and related to 'six' because it is the merging of *two trinities*; two bodies, two spirits, two souls, totalling *six* emanations.

From the six there is only one logical place to go next...

Chapter 22

The Seven

In the *Corpus Hermeticum*, a collection of texts attributed to Hermes Trismegistus, there is a reference to the "seven rulers" who govern the cosmos. These rulers are often referred to as the "seven planetary gods" or the "seven planetary spheres" in astrology and other esoteric traditions.

The seven rulers are associated with the seven visible *planets* known to ancient Greek and Roman astrologers by different names and still present in the sky today for all to see:

1. Kronos (Saturn)

2. Zeus (Jupiter)

3. Ares (Mars)

4. Helios (Sun)

5. Aphrodite (Venus)

6. Hermes (Mercury)

7. Selene (Moon)

Each of these are associated with certain qualities and aspects of consciousness, and they are thought to influence the lives and destinies of individuals according to the placement on their astrological birth chart.

Saturn (Kronos)

Time, limitation, discipline, responsibility, authority structure, karma, consequences, wisdom and maturity;

Jupiter (Zeus)

Expansion, growth, abundance, mercy, learning, generosity, compassion, faith, optimism, luck and fortune;

Mars (Ares)

Energy, masculinity, action, determination, persistence, courage, competitiveness, anger, aggression, sexuality and passion;

Venus (Aphrodite)

Love, beauty, sensuality, pleasure, maidenhood, fertility, aesthetics, artistry, diplomacy, cooperation, sociable and charming;

Mercury (Hermes)

Communication, intellect, writing, speech, rhetoric, science, technology, music, travel, alchemy, magic and mischief;

Moon (Selene)

Emotions, intuition, nurturing, motherhood, transformation, reflection, contemplation, subconscious mind, mysteries;

Sun (Helios)

Vitality, life force, identity, awareness, self-expression illumination, creativity, leadership, success and victory.

The number 7 is of central significance in alchemy and all spiritual science. A set of seven can be called a Septenary. There are many intriguing septenaries in our realm, of which we shall list but a taster:

- 7 days of the week
- 7 days of creation
- 7 luminaries/visible planets
- 7 colours in the rainbow
- 7 notes in the music scale
- 7 metals of alchemy
- 7 steps of transformation
- 7 continents
- 7 seas
- 7 chakras
- 7 holes in the head
- 7 divisions of the brain
- 7 chambers in the heart
- 7 parts to the cornea and the inner ear
- 7 systems of the body
- 7 wonders of the world
- 7 rays of divine light
- 7 cardinal sins
- 7 cardinal virtues
- And so on

There are many more notable septenaries that could be listed, but we will leave those for the reader to discover by self study. My favourite is '7 holes in the head', 2 eyes, 2 nostrils, 2 ears and 1 mouth totalling 7 holes, a simple fact that seems to go almost completely unnoticed by and large.

Everyone knows they have 10 fingers and toes, but nobody knows they have 7 holes in their head. When you add those to the 2 other holes 'down under', we get a total of 9 holes in the body, one for each of the pure numbers, and this could well be the occult reason for the 9 holes in a round of Golf. Of course women have a 10th hole because they are 'holier' than men.

But sticking with the 7 for now, the main septenary we are concerned with here is the 7 Steps of Transformation. seven natural processes that relate specifically to the 4 elements and the 3 principles, for 4+3=7.

Seven symbolises the union of spirit and matter, since it combines the Trinity, 3-fold nature of spirit (God), with matter, the 4-fold nature of the elements (man). The 7 steps of transformation provide a recipe for skilfully combining spirit and matter into something unique and pure.

A quality work of art has the pure spirit of the artist infused throughout it, in every microscopic detail. Consider a sculpture, which at one point is just a lump of rock, but after several days of hard labour, focused effort and craftsmanship, with elemental tools to carve, smooth, and polish the rock face, it becomes a timeless marvel capturing the essence of its inspiration.

Alchemy is about the redemption of spirit from matter and the infusion of spirit into matter. The dictum *solve et coagula* means to dissolve and coagulate, to break things down and put them back together again, the essence of chemistry, creativity and all technological progress.

The 7 steps of transformation are real physical processes that are constantly occurring within our mind and bodies, and within nature and the cosmos. They are so common that we hardly even notice them. They are used in all forms of industry and we work with them every day without even thinking about it.

The Hermetical Triumph, or The Victorious Philosopher's
Stone, by P. Hanet (1723)

The 7 alchemical processes are symbolised abstractly in the above image going up the centre column, from the fire pit at the base:

1.Calcination (heating, roasting, pulverising);

2.Dissolution (dissolving, washing, swirling);

3.Separation (filtering, organising, sifting);

4.Conjunction (combining, unifying, integrating);

5.Fermentation (digestion, death of matter, release of spirit);

6.Distillation (refinement, purification of spirit);

7.Coagulation(solidification, crystallisation, manifestation).

Let us better understand them by looking at some of the most mundane applications. The first four processes are used in the making of a cup of tea.

1) the picking and drying of the tea leaves (calcination)

2) the dissolving of the leaves in hot water (dissolution)

3) the removal of the unwanted teabag (separation)

4) the blending of milk and sugar into it (conjunction)

These are not theories, nor speculations, nor hypothetical nor beyond the realm of human senses, this is as grounded as you can get. You literally did alchemy already today when you made your morning brew.

The first four processes correspond with the elements. Calcination is the application of Fire; dissolution is to dissolve in Water; separation is a power of the Air; conjunction corresponds with Earth, since it is the combination and integration of the saved elements from separation. Earth is the product of the combined action of Fire, Air, and Water.

The last 3 processes in the 7 steps are more subtle, but nevertheless are commonly occurring in nature, in industry and the human body. They correspond with the three primes:

5) Fermentation - Sulphur - Soul

6) Distillation - Mercury - Spirit

7) Coagulation - Salt - Body

Fermentation is a death and rebirth process, since it involves the breakdown or death of organic material such as sugars, and the subsequent production of spirit, or alcohol. Material death produces spirit, and it corresponds with sulphur via the sulphurous gases produced by digestion and necrosis.

In the production of beer and wine, fermentation is the process that makes the money, before that it's just barley water and grape juice. Fermentation is initiated with a 'starter', in this case Yeast, which consumes the sugars and produces alcohol (fiery water) and carbon dioxide (earthy air). The art of brewing is in finding the perfect balance of these components.

In the production of purified alcoholic spirits like Whiskey and Vodka, the sixth process of Distillation is employed. Here, the product of the fermentation is gently heated in a distiller, which causes the most volatile and subtle spiritual essences to separate and rise up the neck of the apparatus, where they are cooled and collected in another container. The collected spirit can be reintroduced to the distiller again and again to increase the purification as much as desired in a feedback loop.

The seventh process, Coagulation, is about embodiment; becoming a body; spirit crystallising into physical reality. In the case of Whiskey, this would be the aging process, where it sits in an oak casket for many years or decades before being bottled for consumption. Many believe alcohol is 'all bad', but it is highly pure and volatile and therefore sensitive to the energy we put into it. This why traditionally we drink for celebration, and clink the glasses together and give a toast to 'good health' or 'cheers.' We are *impregnating* the spirit before we consume it. Drinking when alone and depressed or anxious will produce bad spirit and is not wise.

The above image[1], known as the *Azoth*, or *The Mercury of the Wise*, is usually one of the first we might encounter when diving into alchemical art. It shows an alchemists face, surrounded by a 7 spoked wheel, indicating the 7 luminaries and the 7 steps of transformation. In his right hand he holds a candle for fire, in the left hand a feather for air, one foot is on water and the other on earth.

The corners of the triangle show the tria prima. Anima (soul), Spiritus (spirit), Corpus (body). The words around the outside of the circle read:

VISITA INTERIORA TERRAE RECTFICANDO INVENIES OCCULTUM LAPIDEM

This Latin phrase is found in several other alchemical emblems. It is commonly translated as '*visit the interior parts of the earth and rectify to find the hidden stone*'.

---

[1] Azothalchemy.org by D.W. Hauck

However there may be some intentional misdirection here. Remember occultists like to conceal knowledge and mislead people who they deem unworthy of the truth. One might get the idea from this to start digging holes, going down mines or exploring caves in some half baked attempt to 'visit the interior parts of the earth', seeking a special stone. No doubt many have.

But the word 'terra' here means 'land' as well as 'earth', so 'visita interiora terrae' is more like 'visit interior lands' meaning the *inner landscape of the mind,* the heart, the *mundus imaginalis,* the dwelling place of your soul, accessible through meditation and altered states of consciousness.

If the purpose of the message was to get people to go underground, it would be *below* or *under* instead of *interior.* Earth is not a planet, it is an element and symbolic of the substance of the human body, since it is said in scripture that man was made from clay, which is water mixed with the dust of the earth.

Ashes to ashes, dust to dust; our body is an earthen vessel carrying the sacred waters of our lifeblood. Interiora terrae is *inner terrain.*

It is *we* - the living human initiate - that is the *Earth* to be *rectified.* Rectification is to make right, to fix, refine or improve, to repent for sins and do better, to seek wisdom. There is a man is at the centre of the image since ultimately the seven steps are a method for the personal transformation of *you,* the alchemist. When we work with materials in the alchemical way we are also transforming ourselves in the process.

So in the seven steps there is this powerful correspondence between the elements, principles and processes of alchemy. They all tie together beautifully and this system can be applied to anything, it's range of application knows no limits, it is a key to mastery of any subject.

Chapter 23
Audio Alchemy

When I first started learning of Alchemy, I was a several years into 'living the dream' as an independent music producer. My initial impression of the seven steps was to realise that they applied perfectly well to my music creation process, so I used this to formulate a seven step process for music production which became known as Audio Alchemy. I taught this system to hundreds of people in retreats and workshops during the years 2016 through 2019, in Hawaii, the US mainland, Australia, and Europe.

As I learned of Alchemy, I realised that every bit of it had a correspondence in music. Alchemy is just as much about music as it is about chemistry or psychology. I came to the inescapable conclusion that music production is a modern form of Alchemy, a kind of Sonic Chemistry.

The various sounds, samples, and waveforms were my chemical ingredients, like the salts, oils, and spirits of the alchemists laboratory. The audio equipment and software plugins were like the various retorts, crucibles and distillation apparatuses; specialised vessels for transformation and purification of audible fire.

I recalled being a young child and having an obsession with drawing chemical contraptions, I would spend hours sketching out these huge complex laboratory set-ups. Spiralling glass tubes, bizarre distillers and mechanical processors, like a mad scientists fantasy. I have been attracted to this kind of work from the youngest age. Something about it just resonated to the core of my being.

Electronic music production is a kind of 'dry alchemy', an application of fire and earth. This discovery was one of the most profound 'ah-ha' moments of my life, it became my whole 'thing' for a while. It was the thrust of inspiration that gave rise to the Audio Alchemy Retreats, and ultimately led to the writing of this book.

Alchemy reveals deep and meaningful connections between music, psychology, and chemistry, as well as giving clear, detailed instructions for personal and spiritual development. A true science of the soul, it is a fountain of inspiration for artists of all kinds.

Realising that Alchemy can be practiced in the medium of music, changed my whole approach to work (and play). It took me many years of experimentation and adjustment to really integrate the knowledge. In 2018 I completed my 'first stage of the work' and built myself an Audio Laboratorium from the ground up; a 5x3m log cabin music studio in my garden at home in Scotland.

As the first stage of Alchemy is called 'the blackening', it is often symbolised by Crows and Ravens, the class of birds known as Corvids. During the first two years settling into my new space, I had Crows and Ravens around me every day, in the tree branches above, on the cabin roof scratching and knocking, on the house roof. It seemed like I could always hear their squawks and squabbles. They were a constant feature in our local air space, I even rescued a baby crow on two occasions.

To acknowledge this, the first piece of music I produced in the new studio was named Corvid Phase (it is commonly mistaken for 'covid phase'). I released this as the first track on the album The Philosopher's Tone in July of 2020. It was the first album I had produced entirely with Audio Alchemy principles every stage of the way. After that, the Corvids disappeared. I tentatively took this as a sign that the first stage of the work - to build the laboratory and carry out a transformation successfully - was complete.

Making the correspondence between alchemy and music is a beautiful and enlightening process, and very much worth doing. Even if you are not interested in making music, it is something of deep cosmic and philosophical significance since life and the universe are fundamentally musical.

Philosophers and mystics have for eons compared the heavens to music, the stars to songs, nature as a chorus or symphony, architecture as 'frozen music', and life as a play or dance. Music permeates every aspect of reality, it's far more than just light entertainment.

Let's now look at music though the lens of the alchemical knowledge gleaned from the previous sections, specifically how it relates to the 7 steps, the 4 elements, the 3 primes, and the 2 genders.

The Elements

Even though music is this abstract thing that exists only momentarily in the vibrations of the air, it still has elements. Everything is reducible to it's core elements.

The table below shows the essential correspondence between the elements of alchemy and the elements of music, their influence on the body, and a description of the character of the sound.

Alchemy	Earth	Water	Air	Fire
Music	Rhythm, Drums, Percussion	Bass, Chords	Melody, Lyrics	Dynamics, Modulation
Influence	Blood pumping, body moving, dancing/ marching	Emotions, Heart feelings	Thoughts, mental stimulation, brain feelings	Energy, Attitude, Soul
Sound	Punchy transient hits with structured noise patterns (hats)	Long notes and deep tones, simple patterns, led by the rhythm	Shorter notes and higher tones, more complex, led by the bass	Movement of energy between the notes, velocity, intensity, style, delivery

The correspondence is made in terms of frequency, and the influence of those frequencies on the body. So the four elements of music, starting at the lowest frequency (most dense) up to the highest frequency (least dense) are:

1. Rhythm (Earth, Body);

2. Bass (Water, Emotions);

3. Melody (Air, Thoughts);

4. Dynamics (Fire, Will).

Rhythm moves the body and bass moves the emotions. When you remove the bass frequencies from a sound, it loses all it's emotional content. Conversely, if you preserve the bass and filter out the high frequencies, you can feel the emotion but you can't hear the information being communicated.

For example, if your upstairs neighbours are fighting, the ceiling dampens the high frequencies enough so you can't tell what's being said, but the low frequencies penetrate and shake the walls so you can still hear the anger and passion in their voices.

In terms of waveforms, the rhythmic element is rough and jagged like the rocks and islands poking out of the ocean, fixed and fractal like 'sonic land' upon which musical architecture can be built.

Bass is long and slow vibrations like the waters that move around the earth, the carrier waves of emotion, the chords and the fundamental frequencies.

Melody is more delicate, intricate, and thoughtful than bass, it spans a much greater range of octaves. It is more free to improvise and bend the rules. Melody is the air element, and nobody does melody better than song birds, the voices of the Air.

Dynamics are the overall movements of the sound, the breath, the modulation, expression and energetics of the performance. This corresponds with the Fire element, the great mover, that which penetrates and modulates all the other elements. Dynamics apply to everything, rhythm, bass, and melodies. This is the role of the conductor in an the orchestra, to lead the dynamics.

The Three Primes

The four elements in music can be reduced into the Three Primes by recognising the essential unity of the Water (bass, chords) and Air (melody, lyrics). These can be grouped together into one, as they represent the notes and tones, the part of the sound that would be written and notated in sheet music. This is the mercurial aspect.

The word 'mercurial' is associated with volatility, quickness, and liveliness, based on the properties of the metal, as well as corresponding to communication, intellect and spirit via the divine messenger. These are all properties of the melodic and lyrical components of music, which is typically quicker, higher in pitch and more lively than the drums. Though it follows the bass, there is a greater range and freedom of expression (volatility), and it is usually communicating a message (the artist being a form of divine messenger).

The rhythm and dynamics are vibrationally distinct from the notes and tones, occupying different frequency bands, and they are much more open to the creative interpretation of the performers. Songs can be expressed in an endless variety of styles while adhering to the notation and lyrical structure. It can be played with drums or without drums, double time or half time, acoustic or electronic, sad or happy, relaxing or intense, etc.

So music, like man, has a 3-fold structure, a body, spirit, and soul. The table below shows the 3 primes and their corresponding principles in music:

Salt/Body	Sulphur/Soul	Mercury/Spirit
Rhythm, Drums	Dynamics, Modulation	Notes, Lyrics
Structure	Energy	Information
Body Movement	Soul Fire	Mental Communication

The fiery aspect is now the sulphur or soul-fire, the movement and energy of the music, the interplay between loud and quiet, the interestingness of the sound, the range of emotional expression, the attitude and timbre of the tones.

The expression of 'hotness' in music is when sounds are saturated with harmonics, the beats are popping and the timing is strict. This is the essence of good dance music; *rhythm and soul.*

When you add lyrics/words into the mix, this adds the *spirit*, some communication, or message, so now we have '*something for your mind, your body, and your soul*'.

Seven Creative Stages

The seven steps define seven stages of the creative process, which can be applied to music or any other art. The basic idea is you start with some raw material, and you work it with increasing levels of purity and refinement until it becomes something beautiful, perfect and complete.

Creation is transformation. The seven steps define the archetypal processes of nature by which all things can be transformed, purified, improved, exalted, made stronger and better, whether it be food, medicine, or music.

Each of these stages of creativity can be discussed in a huge amount of detail. In the Audio Alchemy retreats, we would spend a whole day focused on each one, diving into the specific musical operations that derive from each of the steps by correspondence, and even that wasn't long enough to do it justice. For the purposes of this book, some associated keywords shall suffice to define the basic system:

1.Calcination; Calibration, tuning, planning, writing;

2.Dissolution; Playing, recording, jamming, flowing;

3.Separation; Filtering, cutting, processing, selecting;

4.Conjunction; Composition, arrangement, structure;

5.Fermentation; Editing, detailing, enlivening, enhancing;

6.Distillation; Refinement, mixing, polishing;

7.Coagulation; Finishing, mastering and releasing.

The key is understanding that the seven alchemical processes are not specific to chemistry, but are symbolic of fundamental processes in the human mind, modes of thought and action that humans carry out with their hands on a daily basis. Alchemy is the basis of *all* work, that is why it's called The Work.

In the first stage, calcination is the preparation of the substance to be transformed. This is the calibration of the musical instruments to be used, selecting the software. It all needs to be defined, tuned and set up, many decisions have to be made before even a single note of music is played. There are infinite possibilities for creativity, so the first step is to reduce the possibilities by deciding on things like tuning, tempo, key, instruments, and even deciding what to sing or play.

Once the first stage is complete, then playing can commence. The act of jamming and coming up with new music on the fly is a state of 'flow', where the impulses of the subconscious are allowed to be expressed without the conscious mind getting in the way.

The limits set by the calibrated musical devices allow for playfulness and a safe-space in which to experiment and make errors. Emotion is transmuted through the feedback loop of playing music and refining it into better and better feeling expressions. So playing is associated with the water element, as is recording, because water has the capacity for memory, it is able to receive and hold vibrations of all kinds.

Separation is using our discernment to pour through the recordings from the Dissolution stage, cut out the unwanted, imperfect takes, and gather together all the golden nuggets. Separation is filtration, the removal of specific frequencies with EQ or compression, the grouping of elements into certain tracks or sections of the composition.

Conjunction is the opposite, it is bringing things together, combining, and integrating the best elements. In music this corresponds with the composition, the structure of the song laid out from beginning to end. The setting of all the parts in their proper place in time and space.

Fermentation corresponds with editing because it is a 'death and rebirth' of sorts, where the composition is broken down and put back together again, infused with new spirit to elevate it to the next level of purity. Unedited compositions can sound very 'raw', not standing up strong on repeated listens, so editing gives it that extra layer of quality beyond what can be achieved in the previous steps.

Distillation corresponds with the mix-down process, where the levels of the musical elements are raised and lowered, agitated and subdued with careful attention until a perfect volume and frequency distribution is achieved. At this stage, the structure of the music is preserved, but the balance between body, soul, and spirit is adjusted to suit the ears of its creator.

Coagulation is the finishing process, which includes mastering and releasing. It's where the 'project' becomes the 'product'. The work is complete and crystallised into a professional quality product which can be unleashed upon the unsuspecting populous. Coagulation would be the printing of CDs or vinyl, or the distribution of the music to stores and streaming sites, etc.

Gender in Music

Gender can be understood in a variety of ways relating to music, but perhaps the primary one to understand is that of the listener and the performer. Listening is feminine/ negative because it is receptive, whereas performing is masculine/positive because it is active. A good musical experience requires good performers *and* good listeners, it's in the union of the two where the magic of the alchemical marriage takes place. People are often quick to judge the quality of an artist's performance, but the quality of the audience and their commitment to listening is also a vital aspect.

In the practice of Ecstatic Dance, there is one DJ for the whole ceremony and people are advised not to talk on the dance floor. This allows for a much deeper and more therapeutic dance experience, with no verbal distractions, nobody shouting nonsense in your ear. It's also wise to have no screens, no visuals, no phones, just mood lighting, helping the dancer to open their third eye and dive within, rather than focusing on external 'false light' symbols and messaging.

For the absolute best most transformational dance experience, everyone should have their shoes off, electrically grounded. The DJ should be on the same level as the crowd, not elevated high up like an idol to be worshipped. In this way, we have a more balanced and grounded relationship between the masculine DJ and the feminine audience. Not domination, but collaboration.

In terms of the sound of the music itself, the two genders are represented in many ways, one of them being the Kick and Snare. The Kick and Snare are the Sun and Moon of groovy music. The Kick is a low frequency pulse that focuses the air into a smooth wave that rolls over the body. The Snare, which means 'trap', is an all-frequency pulse that scrambles the air, lights up the whole range of sonic attention. White noise is the audio equivalent of white light, it contains all frequencies and so drowns-out the individual tones, as white light drowns out individual colours (useful for jamming signals).

Kick is masculine because it's a pulse of pure frequency, where as a snare/trap is feminine because it's a container of many frequencies.

A simple 8th note drum beat will consist of kick and snare drums marking the count of the music; the kick lands on the 1 and the 3 and the snare lands on the 2 and the 4, like Michael Jackson's 'Billie Jean.' This is the natural way to play beats, it makes no sense to reverse the order, the kick must come first or the beat will be 'out of step'. We are 'kicked into the trap' not 'trapped into the kick'.

The genders reveal themselves in the numbering system also:

- Odd numbers 1,3,5,7,9 are masculine;

- Even numbers 2,4,6,8 are feminine.

The words 'odd' and 'even' correspond to 'Adam' and 'Eve'. Adam was the first man so number 1, and Eve number 2.

Also the female is 'divisible by 2' since they are uniquely capable of giving birth to child, so all even numbers are feminine.

The male is the seed, so 'female' also contains 'male' within it, just as 'woman' contains 'man', and the number 2 contains the number 1.

Men Are From ...

Mars (Ares) and Venus (Aphrodite) are strongly gendered archetypes, being the masculine god of war and the feminine goddess of beauty and fertility, and as such they have a particular musical correspondence which we observe again and again in film and game music.

Most stories involve some amount of action or fighting, and some amount of romance, and the music for those scenes are quite different. Action scenes invoke the martian energy with pounding drums and high-octane frequencies to get the blood pumping and the iron flowing through the veins. Mars is marching music, mars is martial arts, mars is war. Military forces take *drums* to the battlefield, not violins.

On the other hand, when the story turns to matters of love and romance, the music becomes softer, gentler, with more sustained tones, out come the violins, the female vocals, the symphonic strings and maybe even a saxophone! Now we begin to feel excited and emotional in a whole other way, the Venusian energy is harmonious and captivating, seductive and luxurious, our desire is activated, and we might even have to cry!

Mercury is gender balanced and in music corresponds with the mental aspect. A lot of electronic music can be described as mercurial, as it's born out of technology and mathematics and waveform synthesis. It's playful and scientific, and also very 'heady'. Mercury also relates to language, lyrics and poetry, the use of the voice for divine messaging.

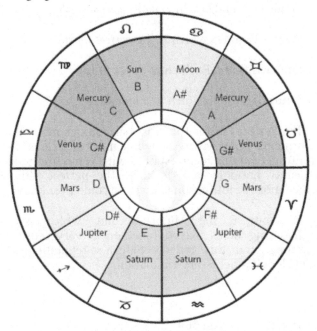

In this image, we have mapped the 12 musical notes to the 12 houses of the zodiac, based on the condition that Aries corresponds with the note G (192Hz).[1] The name of the planetary ruler of each house is also included. The Sun and Moon only rule one house each and so are represented by a single neighbouring notes B and A#, but from this we can obtain a musical interval representing each of the other five luminaries.

Musical intervals of two or more notes have a unique emotional quality, unlike individual notes which have no particular emotion attached when played in isolation. So from playing and listening to these intervals we can get a

---

[1] 192Hz is an octave of the colour of deep red. Red corresponds with Aries as it's the first colour in the octave of visible light.

sense for the emotional quality of the planets;

Mercury is C and A, which is the *major sixth.*

Venus is C and G which is the *perfect fifth.*

Mars is D and G which is the *perfect fourth.*

Jupiter is D and F which is *minor third.*

Saturn is E and F which is *minor second.*

The Perfect Fifth is the most harmonious interval and the principle upon which the whole musical scale is based, it is fitting then that it corresponds with Venus, the goddess of beauty harmony and fertility. The perfect fifth has birthed more beautiful songs than we could ever know.

In contrast, the Minor Second, which is two neighbouring notes played together, is very tense and unsettling, and this reflects Saturn's reputation as a malevolent but necessary emanation.

The 432 and The 369

The specific reference frequency that defines the pitch and range of available notes of an instrument is called *tuning*, and the principles by which the notes are spaced is called *temperament* or *intonation*.

The international standard of musical tuning since 1938 is a 12-tone equal temperament system based on a tuning of A4 = 440Hz. All digital and electronic instruments come tuned to this scale by default, and acoustic instruments are mostly made for it.

Equal Temperament (ET) means that the octave is split into 12 equal portions called semi-tones. The octaves are obtained by doubling and halving the reference frequency, so

A3 = 220Hz, A2 = 110Hz, A1 = 55 Hz, A5 = 880Hz etc.

The values of the semi-tones are obtained by multiplying the reference frequency by a number called the **'twelfth root of 2'** (approximately 1.059463...).

So to calculate A#4, the first semi-tone up from A4, we would do as follows:

440 x 1.059... = 466.16 Hz

And this has to be truncated to two decimal places. Then to calculate B4, the next semi-tone up, we would multiply again in sequence:

B4 = 466.16 x 1.059 = 493.66 Hz

and so on up the scale until we have the full set of musical frequencies.

This 440ET scale sounds reasonably acceptable, probably every song you've ever loved has been made with these frequencies, but the problem is that the 'twelfth root of two' is an **irrational number**, it cannot be expressed as a whole number ratio so there will always be some dissonance and noise introduced when playing chords and melodies built upon this number.

True harmony requires the use of precise whole number ratios, so that frequencies and waves fit together *exactly*. In 440ET, all the frequencies, except for the octaves of A, are approximated, truncated irrational numbers. As of December 2013, the twelfth root of two was calculated to *20 billion digits!!*

So you see, equal temperament can never be truly harmonic because of its reliance on the irrational 'twelfth root of two'. Harmonic intervals are based on whole number ratios like 2/1 or 3/2, not irrational multipliers or square roots. Such a scale is said to be *unjust*.

It's equivalent to building a house with bricks that are 1.0594 ft long, each new brick would introduce small errors in the measurements, and the walls of the house would end up as an irrational length, where things don't line up properly.

The touted benefit of equal temperament is the ability to transpose melodies into any key (called 'key modulation') and have them sound harmonically the same. With non-equal temperaments, each key produces a slightly different scale so melodies are more dependent on the key they were originally composed in.

The so-called 'perfect fifth' is actually not perfect in ET, playing for example C and G together does produce a slight dissonant beating as the waves misalign by an error factor of 2%. This is very much audible to the trained ear.

The word 'harmony' means 'joining', it is the *precise* joining together of waveforms to create resonance or consonance. Deviation from harmony creates distortion and dissonance, and though a small amount can be pleasant, it should not be a built-in feature of the standard musical scale.

The ET440 scale is imperfect and dissonant on a subtle level, it is a distortion of the natural musical scale which is inherent the god-given number system itself. ET440 is to music what big pharma is to medicine; it's a flawed, artificial and industrially enforced standard which is far inferior to what is provided by nature. The reasons for the international standards body to choose 440Hz as the reference frequency for A4 are not exactly clear, though there is much speculation on the subject we will refrain from indulging in that here.

History does seems to show a trend of increasing musical pitch over the centuries, with A4 being as low as 374Hz in the 1700s, up to 415-430Hz in the 1800s, even up to 452.5Hz at one point. Mozart's piano we are told was tuned to 421.6Hz.

High pitched tones mean more tension, more excitement, just as when we tune up a guitar we have to literally tighten the strings, tune it too high and the strings will snap. Conversely, tuning down is more relaxing but if we go too far it feels flabby and deflating, and low notes can't be reached so easily.

There are many ways to construct a scale, technically there are infinite ways, an instrument designer is free to tune it however he desires. But there is an optimal temperament that is not born from human calculation, experimentation or convention. One that simply exists in the universe, coded into the natural number system itself.

Here we will show how the number 432 is the only natural choice for the musical reference frequency A4.

Natural tuning is based quite simply on the two most harmonious intervals, the octave and the perfect fifth. In mathematical terms, this means *doubling* (2/1) and *tripling* (3/1), as well as halving (1/2).

We start at the beginning, with number 1, then apply the operations of doubling and tripling, like so:

Doubling: 1, 2, 4, 8, 16, 32, 64, 128, 256, 512, 1024, 2048 ...

Tripling: 1, 3, 9, 27, 81, 243, 729, 2187 ...

Tripling produces the Perfect Fifth one octave up from the root note, so by tripling we can get reference frequencies for all notes, and by doubling we can get all their octaves.

It is best viewed in tabular form:

C	G	D	A	E	B
1	1.5	2.25	3.375	5.0625	7.59375
2	3	4.5	6.75	10.125	15.1875
4	6	9	13.5	20.25	30.375
8	12	18	27	40.5	60.75
16	24	36	54	81	121.5
32	48	72	108	162	243
64	96	144	216	324	486
128	192	288	432	648	972
256	384	576	864	1296	1944
512	768	1152	1728	2592	3888
1024	1536	2304	3456	5184	7776
2048	3072	4608	6912	10368	15552
4096	6144	9216	13824	20736	31104

In the table we start in the top left, the key of C is set to correspond with the number 1 and by doubling down the column this gives us all of it's octaves. In the audible range, the lowest C sub-bass would be 32Hz, but all octaves of the number 1 are technically harmonics of c.

Taking the C=1, and multiplying by (3/2), we get our perfect fifth G = 1.5. From there we go down the column by doubling, and this gives all the octaves of G.

Continuing in this way, we can obtain all the numerical values for the 12 musical keys. Looking at the column for A, we see that the number 432 is right smack in the middle of the table, completely naturally, and by no choice or convention imposed by any man or group. All the note frequencies are natural harmonic numbers or whole number ratios, no truncation or approximation, no square roots or dissonant intervals.

In order to tune a guitar in this way, it's important to realise that the standard frets are built for ET spacing, but we can nevertheless tune the open strings to pure numbers using a frequency based tuner, from lowest to highest:

E = 81Hz

A = 108Hz

D = 144Hz

G = 192Hz

B = 243Hz

E = 324Hz

There's a few things to notice about these numbers. We can see two permutations of 432 in the B and E values of 243 and 324.

A is 108, which is two octaves down from 432, and D = 144, which is 432/3.

If we add up the digits in each frequency value in the table, and reduce them to a single digit (the digital root), we find that almost all of them add up to 3, 6, and 9. For example:

81, 108, 144, 243, 324 and 432 all add up to 9

In the column for the key of G, taking the digital root of each frequency, we see that the octaves oscillate between 3 and 6:

1.5(=6), 3, 6, 12(=3), 24(=6), 48(=12=3), 96(=17=6) ...

The notable exception is the starting key of C, which when we take the digital root of each octave, we get more complex pattern of numbers:

1, 2, 4, 8, 16(=7), 32(=5), 64(=10=1), 128(=11=2) ...

The repeating pattern here is 124875, 124875 ... it's going around all the other numbers except for 3, 6 and 9.

So in general then, when doubling the number series and taking the digital root, we find that the values always stick to one of these three patterns;

1.   Reduce to 9 every time

2.   Oscillate between 3 and 6

3.   Repeat the cycle of 1-2-4-8-7-5-1-2-4-8-7-5 ...

This gets into the field of *Vortex Based Mathematics*, which was pioneered by a man named Marko Rodin.

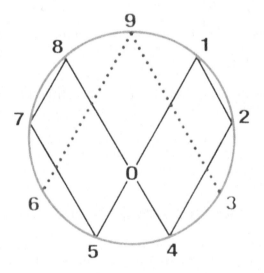

Rodin calls this image 'the fingerprint of God', or 'God's petroglyph'. His work is very number heavy and can be hard to follow along with but the math is sound. It's all based on the 'doubling circuit', which is also 'the octave' in music.

The glyph is a very fundamental pattern in nature and deserves to be studied and contemplated deeply. It expresses how energy manifests and propagates out of the aether by the principle of vortex dynamics.

Based on the doubling circuit of the natural numbers, they are assigned electric and magnetic properties:

1, 7, 4 = positive electric

2, 8, 5 = negative electric

3, 6, 9 = magnetic

Seeing the numbers grouped this way, and being something of a 'frequency aficionado', we may notice how they look a lot like the much touted Solfeggio tones. Indeed, the Solfeggio frequencies are all permutations of these three groups of numbers:

Ut: 396Hz (magnetic)

Re: 417Hz (+)

Mi: 528Hz (-)

Fa: 639Hz (magnetic)

Sol: 741Hz (+)

La: 852Hz (-)

Ti: 963Hz (magnetic)

Sound healers who work with these tones in the form of tuning forks and crystal bowls report powerful and specific healing benefits[1].

Eileen McKusik has spent nearly three decades studying the anatomy of the human biofield with tuning forks, mapping the locations of specific diseases and conditions in the electromagnetic field around the body. Her work shows how the source of disease is often held as distortions in the aether field surrounding us, and can be healed with specific tones and frequencies.

---

[1] Tuning the Human Biofield, by Eileen Day McKusik

Putting it all together then, we can see from the table that the notes G, D, A, E, B (and F), all reduce to 3, 6 or 9, and are therefore **magnetic**. And the note C, which goes through the whole cycle of 1-2-4-8-7-5 is **electric**.

So this natural 432 music scale can be said to be *highly magnetic* and *just,* whereas the man-made industrial standard of 440ET is *highly electric,* and *unjust* due to the truncation and approximation of frequencies. There is also creeping imprecision in the doubling such that intervals are not harmonic. The **perfect** fifth is not even implemented perfectly in ET, and so it surely cannot be deemed to be a satisfactory musical scale.

Just as magnetic fields are generated by electric currents, magnetic frequencies are generated the electric frequencies (all the notes were derived from C=1, by tripling and doubling). Light waves have a magnetic and electric component woven together in exactly this way. Fire is the prime driver of movement and manifestation.

When we take 432x432 we get 186,624 which is the approximate value of the speed of light in miles per second, so people say 432 is a 'harmonic of the speed of light'.

We also find that 432 is one of the most harmonic numbers in its range, with 20 divisors: 1, 2, 3, 4, 6, 8, 9, 12, 16, 18, 24, 27, 36, 48, 54, 72, 108, 144, 216 and 432.

　　　　4 is positive electric

　　　　3 is magnetic

　　　　2 is negative electric

So in the combination 432 we have a highly divisible number with all 3 electromagnetic traits and a balance of masculine and feminine energies. Individually they are symbolic of the 4 elements, 3 principles and 2 genders, and when put together they equal 9 and produce a perfect musical scale and the speed of light.

The Philosopher's Tone

The image below is from a 16th century text by german alchemist Michael Maier[1]. It contains one of the most commonly cited symbols for the Philosopher's Stone.

We see an alchemist holding a large compass and drawing a circle on a dilapidated stone wall. The symbol consists of an outer circle with a triangle inside, then a square inside the triangle with a second circle inside the square. The top of the square is aligned with the horizon line of the outer circle, and a man and woman stand naked inside the inner circle.

If we take just the basic shapes, we see there is two circles, one triangle, and one square. The shapes are symbolic of numbers via their essential geometry. Square represents 4, triangle represents 3, and circles represent one, the whole. And there is TWO of them. So there it is again, **432**, cast into this ancient symbol for the stone.

---

[1] Atalanta Fugiens (1617), by Michael Maier

Back in 2018, being increasingly convinced that alchemy is music, and music is alchemy, I made the connection that 'philosopher's stone' is homophonic with 'philosopher's *tone*', and started to wonder if maybe the stone is a *frequency*.

How fitting then, when I learned that 432Hz tuning was known as Scientific Pitch or *Philosopher's Pitch*. In music the words *pitch* and *tone* are often used interchangeably, even though they are technically distinct. Given everything we've learned about it, 432Hz can justifiably be referred to the **Philosopher's Tone**.

The correspondence and synchronicities between alchemy and music have continued to unfold, year after year, as I have walked this path. The contents of this book are only a taster of what is possible. I hope to have proven that music can be an alchemical practice that is just as legitimate as any other kind. Indeed some[1] have told me that they believe music to be *the highest form of alchemy*.

It certainly can be highly potent medicine when done and delivered properly, and the ability of music to persist and endure through time is something only comparable to gold. Music is immortal, timeless, infinitely reproducible. It can't be tarnished or degraded. Once the quality is established it radiates through time like a crystal of sound in the cavern of the collective consciousness.

Though I have spent many years making wordless dance music, I do concede that the most potent and powerful type of music comes from the human voice, utilising lyrics, rhyme, and harmonics. Songs that people can sing and voices can share, songs that take on new meaning at different stages in life. When I was a young fool I only heard the sounds, the frequencies, but now I'm a wee bit wise, I hear the lyrics, the meaning, the symbolism, and it's all felt much more deeply.

---

[1] Including the legendary Dr. Barre Lando of Alfavedic.com

Chapter 24

The Cosmic Vortex

With all that has been said regarding the beauty and veracity of alchemy, and exposing the occult nature and patent absurdity of scientism, it would be unbecoming not to end this book with a discussion of the bigger picture, the grand unifying principle that ties it all together. I am talking of course, about **The Vortex**.

Though well within the realm of conventional physics, the vortex or toroid is quietly occulted from the curriculum. Its mentioned but its significance is played down. In all my 10 years of physics education I hardly even heard about it. Fluid dynamics was a topic for applied math students, not physicists (strangely enough).

We are told there is a toroidal magnetic field vortex around 'planet earth', and also around every molecule, atom and particle, even around the human heart. But it is treated as a secondary phenomenon, a consequence of the *real stuff,* the spinning material of atoms, particles and planets. But what if, instead, the 'real stuff' is a secondary consequence of the vortex?

Physicists, being solely focused on the physical, are always seeking a material solution to a spiritual problem. Aether provides a spiritual source from which all material manifestation results through the dynamic power of the vortex.

The aether, as we've discussed, is impregnated with both masculine and feminine genders and so is thus capable of creation, by setting up electrical polarities or pressure differentials which generate vortices. This idea is wrapped up in the atomic theory where it is said that hydrogen consists of a single electron (f) and proton (m) in a dynamic relationship called a 'wave-function' which is able to take many different shapes depending on the energy of the spin.

The atomists have invented hypothetical spinning particles to be the material driving force of the immaterial vortex, because they cannot accept the principle of aether, which implies the opposite.

We observe vortices all the time; water moves in a spiral fashion down a riverbed, and most commonly we see this when it's draining down a sink hole or when we stir it. In the air we see dust devils, hurricanes, and tornados. There are also vortices in the earth, which are the trees, plants, crystals, flowers, and fruits.

Consider the water vortex, the whirlpool. Though it is separate and distinct from the rest of the water, with its own size, shape, position, speed, power. It is still part of the ocean. It is individual and unique, but also still connected, at one with the whole body of water.

The vortex demonstrates how something can be perceptually distinct, free to move and interact but without being disconnected from the medium that manifested it.

A vortex can be viewed in many different ways, from inside, outside, above, and below. It can be upward flowing or downward flowing or both, it can be referred to as a toroidal field or a tube-torus, which describes the shape of the field around the vortex.

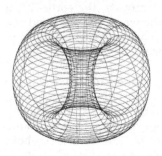

Tube torus from outside (donut)

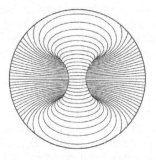

Tube torus from inside (dog nose)

This effect is utilised in electrical appliances in the forms of coils, where current is fed through a spiralling wire, producing a toroidal magnetic field which is used in transformers, speakers, motors, etc. It also works the other way, if a coil is introduced to a magnetic field it begins conducting current in proportion to the strength of the field.

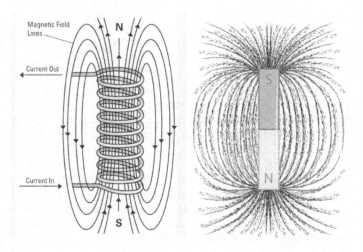

If we put a cup of water onto a magnetic stirrer, and set it spinning, the first thing we observe is a small dimple forming in the waters surface. It starts twisting and gets deeper and narrower while spinning around until it reaches its lowest point at the bottom of the jar. This opening in the waters surface is a **mouth.** The vortex has a mouth, and if we listen to it as the water spins around, we will hear that it sounds just like a human gargling water in their throat. The vortex has a **throat**.

At the bottom of the vortex is the **tail**, where all the energy is channeled into a narrow point and squeezed down and out in a divergent twirl before ascending back up the sides toward the mouth to go spiralling down around the circuit again. The motion of the vortex is both *convergent* and *divergent*, it converges inward top to bottom then it flips and begins to diverge outward as it comes back up.

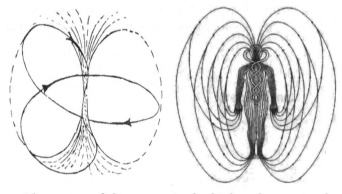

The centre of the vortex is the highest harmonic, the rapidly spinning core of the structure. In the human being this corresponds to the spinal column, the Ida and Pingala spiral channels represented by the two snakes in the Caduceus.

The mouth of a vortex is quite stable whereas the tail is more chaotic. It whips around and is unpredictable and wily, like a python being held by its end. This is the origin of our lower animal nature, which is ultimately to be tamed by the higher consciousness in the head.

A wise Seer once said to me '*every living thing is a mouth*'. It all makes sense in light of the vortex. We are each formed from an aether vortex, which is a mouth and a tail with a throat in between. We are a mouth, and all experience is food, whether it be material sustenance, words, images or sensations, it's all food for the microcosmic vortex that we are.

This profound truth is most exemplified by the serpent, who, without any arms, legs, wings or fins, is basically just a mouth with a long throat and tail. The snake moves in a spiral fashion, it coils and weaves, reflecting the dynamics of the aether vortex that sustains it.

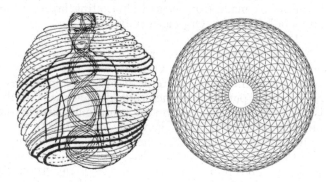

The spiralling dynamics of the vortex, when seen from above produces a pattern that is the grid from which all flower designs emerge. A flow-er is an expression of a vortex in motion, as are fruits and trees, and even seashells. All living things are a mouth, and all mouths are a vortex.

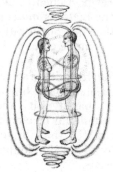

In the case of a whirlpool or a tornado, the vortex is of such magnitude that we can see it and feel it's power. There are also vortices in the aether which are below our sensory threshold, subtle energy currents that surround rocks, plants and crystals, that gently stimulate and nourish other living vortices in the vicinity.

The art and science of Orgonite is about fabricating objects which are capable of producing a subtle harmonising aether vortex. In the original experiments by Wilhelm Reich[1], it was demonstrated that there is an energetic effect from combining organic and inorganic materials together in close proximity. The earliest example being a box made from nested alternating layers of steel and wool, called an 'Orgone accumulator'.

Reich believed he was generating a new exotic type of energy which he called 'Orgone.' We know now that scientists in those days were desperate to claim discovery of some new particle that they can call their own, but there is no such thing in creation as an orgone particle, there have never been any genuine discoveries of any 'fundamental particles.' The energy he was observing was due to *vortices in the aether.* People have equated orgone with 'chi' and 'prana', the vital energy of eastern esoteric traditions, but again, there are no special particles, its all the same thing, the aether vortex is the life-force energy.

Orgonite, as the name suggests, is a type of man made stone that generates this energy. At its most basic, it is said to consist of 50% metal particles (the smaller the better) and 50% resin. Alchemically, the resin is *feminine and organic,* and the metal is *masculine and inorganic.* So mixing them together in a 50/50 ratio and coagulating them in a mould is an example of an *alchemical wedding.*

Reich made no secret of the fact that his orgone energy was related to the human sexual energy, and he chose the name based off the word 'orgasm.' Given our understanding of alchemy and the gender in everything, we can see that 'orgone' is just a word for the vortex produced by the conjunction of masculine and feminine materials.

---

[1] The Orgone Accumulator Handbook, by James DeMeo.

Like the aether itself, orgonite has a balance of masculine and feminine components and so is able to produce a living vortex in response to being charged with energy. It can be from sunlight, ambient heat, or even the EMF's emitted from electronic devices, but the energy that goes in is conditioned and purified, and released in a subtle energy vortex around the object.

Though it can be hard to measure this effect with conventional tech tools, one way is to freeze a jar of water with a piece of orgonite underneath it. Put a jar of water in the freezer, place an orgonite pyramid in the shelf below, leave it for a day. When you take it out, you will observe evidence of the upward twisting motion in the freezing patterns of the water.

Orgonite is often made in the shape of a pyramid, and pyramids have been shown to produce vortex energy purely by virtue of their shape. The pyramid (and the cone) mimic the basic shape of a vortex, where the energy is concentrated toward a point at the tip. Single terminated Quartz crystals also produce a vortex emanating from the tip, so these are put into the tip of the pyramid to amplify the effect. Copper coils also produce a vortex, so these are often wrapped around the Quartz crystal to combine with and amplify the effect even more.

Coil-wrapped single terminated Quartz point in tip for triple vortex combination

Layer of crystals and gemstones to purify and harmonise

Resin and metal pieces in a 50-50 mixture for the perfect alchemical marriage

One of our Orgonite pyramids on the living room window sill, with a small dome in front

The vortex is the principle that unites the above and below, providing a dynamic model that fits the microcosm (man) and the macrocosm (creation) and all the various components thereof. The vortex even unites both the 'flat earth' and 'globe earth' perspectives. In both cases, there is acknowledged to be a toroidal magnetic field around the earth and all 'heavenly bodies'.

 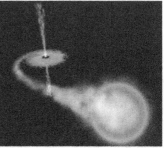

'Planet earth' with magnetic vortex *'Black hole' cannibalising a star*

In the heliocentric globe model, the spinning planet is deemed to be the generator of the toroidal vortex, which 'deflects the particles' from the 'solar wind', but in the geocentric perspective, life manifests *from the vortex* on the *plane of inertia*, which is a level surface in the centre of the torus where the energy is balanced.

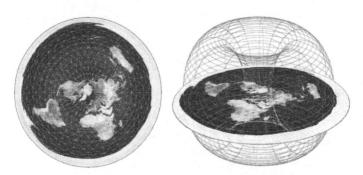

Flat map with toroidal geometry superimposed

In galactic astrophysics, they talk of the *Accretion Disc,* which is a *disc of matter* said to form in the *plane of inertia* around a 'spinning black hole' (black sun?) which produces a gravitational vortex that sucks in matter from nearby stars. They even talk of 'galactic cannibalism', where one galaxy eats another by this same process.

Unsurprisingly, we've been misled about galaxies as well. The word 'galactic' stems from 'lactic' meaning 'milky', since it refers to the parts of the sky that are milky in appearance, a diffuse white cloud where individual stars cannot be visually resolved (like the 'milky way'). There are visible 'swirls' in the night sky, indicative of heavenly vortices, but once we have the knowledge that gravity is bunk, there is no longer any reason to believe that these milky areas consist of billions of alien solar systems all separated by astronomical distances in a 'galaxy far far away.' Such a position is no longer tenable.

Of course we cannot discount the idea of other worlds altogether. It stands to reason that if there is one creation, there may be more. And despite what the bible says about the firmament, there is no evidence yet of an impenetrable glass wall where the world ends. There could very well be lands beyond Antartica, larger harmonics of the toroid.

The torus field is encoded into the golden ratio through the 'golden spiral' and greek symbol *Phi,* which is a column and a circle combined, a '1' and a '0', an 'I' and an 'O', a line and a curve, a phallus and womb. The masculine and feminine in perfect alchemical union.

A α = Phallus & sperm

alpha

Ω ω = Womb & breasts

omega

The vortex unites the masculine and feminine, and the physical and spiritual. It provides a model for the principle of karma and consequence, the idea that 'we reap what we sow' or 'what goes around comes around' or 'to give is to receive.' All of these ideas make perfect sense in a vortex because everything we put out comes back to us in one form or another, like a boomerang, but modified by the journey in some way.

The Hermetic principle 'as above so below, as within so without' also makes more sense in a toroid. Indeed all seven Hermetic axioms from the Kybalion can be derived from contemplation of the essential energetic structure and function of the vortex.

Finally, many scientists are now awakening to the fact that the beating heart is *not a pump*, as we have been told, but a *vortex*, that spins the blood rapidly in the centre of the chest to keep it structured and vitalised. The vortex is the key to tying all of this knowledge together and applying it in your own life.

There is much *much* more that could be said about the vortex, the genders, Hermeticism, and all of the topics in this book, but at some point I just have to stop writing.

I hope this has been an enlightening and informative journey, dear reader. Thank you for making it to the end. May the golden rays of wisdom forever illuminate your path. Let this work help inspire a new alchemical renaissance, where man and woman, science and spirituality, governments and individuals, can all work together in peaceful collaboration under the eternal guidance of truth and wisdom.

So mote it be.

Made in United States
North Haven, CT
10 January 2025

64265382R00147